INTRODUCTION

ULI is pleased to publish this commemorative edition of the first *Community Builders Handbook*, which came out in 1947. The handbook presents the dialogues of the Community Builders Council, which was formed in 1944 at the behest of renowned Country Club District developer J.C. Nichols, who was concerned about the problems facing American cities. The small group of men who formed the Community Builders Council focused on identifying those elements that make up lasting, livable communities, that ultimately make cities better places to live, and that would help guide community building during the fast-changing postwar years and the suburban building boom.

The handbook created a bit of a stir in the real estate and homebuilders world, receiving excellent reviews in the daily press and in real estate and planning publications. The *New York Times* listed it as one of the outstanding books of the year in the planning and realty field. Subsequently, the handbook was expanded and revised several times and five different editions were published. Over the past 25 years, the handbook evolved into the Community Builders Handbook Series with a group of specialized development handbooks, beginning with the *Industrial Development Handbook,* published in 1975. Today, the series is published as the ULI Development Handbook Series.

J.C. Nichols was well known for his approach to community building, reflected in some of his innovations for the Country Club District in Kansas City, Missouri. For example, he established comprehensive deed restrictions for the Country Club District, which included the control of land use, and which established a minimum cost of dwellings, setback lines, building projections, open space, outbuildings, billboards, etc. He also created a "homes association" to provide for owner support of upkeep and maintenance.

This book is intended to honor the work of the founding members of ULI, especially that of J.C. Nichols. ULI is reprinting the book to coincide with the awarding of the first-ever Urban Land Institute J.C. Nichols Prize for Visionary Urban Development.

Please note that this imprint is a replica of the 1947 edition and is intended as a historical document. Therefore, the reader may find occasional language use and concepts that would be considered inappropriate or offensive by today's standards. By reprinting this book, ULI is not intending to endorse or comment on any of the principles outlined in the text. Rather, it is celebrating the contributions made by these pioneering development professionals.

Richard M. Rosan
President
ULI–the Urban Land Institute
September 2000

THE
COMMUNITY BUILDERS
HANDBOOK

●

Prepared

By the

Community Builders' Council

of the

Urban Land Institute

1947

●

1737 K STREET, N.W.
WASHINGTON 6, D. C.

ULI Catalog Number: C61
ISBN: 0-87420-844-0

Copyright 2000 by ULI–the Urban Land Institute
1025 Thomas Jefferson Street, N.W.
Suite 500 West
Washington, D.C. 20007

First Edition and First Printing 1947
Revised Printing 1948
Second or J.C. Nichols Memorial Edition and Second Revised Printing 1950
Third or The Members Edition and Third Revised Printing 1954
Fourth Revised Printing 1956
Fourth or The Executive Edition and Fifth Revised Printing 1960
Sixth Printing 1965
Fifth or Anniversary Edition and Seventh Revised Printing 1968
Eighth Printing 1971
Ninth Printing 1973
Tenth Printing 1973
Commemorative Printing 2000

PRINTED IN THE UNITED STATES OF AMERICA

Analyzing a Plan at a Council Session

NEWTON C. FARR, *President*
Urban Land Institute

J. C. NICHOLS, *Chairman*
Community Builders' Council

Members of the Community Builders' Council

J. C. NICHOLS, *Chairman*, Kansas City, Missouri

W. P. ATKINSON,
Oklahoma City, Okla.

DAVID D. BOHANNON,
San Mateo, Cal.

JUDSON BRADWAY,
Detroit, Mich.

JAMES A. BRITTON,
Greenfield, Mass.

FRITZ BURNS,
Los Angeles, Cal.

CYRIL DEMARA,
Toronto, Canada

L. F. EPPICH,
Denver, Colo.

NEWTON C. FARR,
Chicago, Ill.

VAN HOLT GARRETT,
Denver, Colo.

ROBERT P. GERHOLZ,
Flint, Mich.

HAROLD JANSS,
Los Angeles, Cal.

ROBERT JEMISON, JR.,
Birmingham, Ala.

CHARLES E. JOERN,
Chicago, Ill.

WILBURN K. KERR,
Columbus, Ohio

CHESTER A. MOORES,
Portland, Ore.

JOHN McC. MOWBRAY,
Baltimore, Md.

E. L. OSTENDORF,
Cleveland, Ohio

HUGH POTTER,
Houston, Texas

HUGH PRATHER,
Dallas, Texas

MAURICE READ,
Berkeley, Cal.

HUGH H. RUSSELL,
Seattle, Wash.

WALTER S. SCHMIDT,
Cincinnati, Ohio

PAUL E. STARK,*
Madison, Wis.

HARRY A. TAYLOR,
East Orange, N. J.

WAVERLY TAYLOR,
Washington, D. C.

CYRUS CRANE WILLMORE,
St. Louis, Mo.

SEWARD H. MOTT, *Executive Director*, Urban Land Institute
MAX S. WEHRLY, *Assistant Director*

---

* Deceased.

●

Editors

SEWARD H. MOTT   MAX S. WEHRLY

Grateful acknowledgment is made to Harold W. Lautner who worked as an editor on preparation of the Handbook in its early stages, and Miss Marion Cox who transcribed and edited the voluminous notes on the proceedings of the Council upon which this volume is based.

Foreword

The Urban Land Institute was organized in December 1939 as an independent, non-profit, research and educational organization in the field of urban planning and land development. Although sponsored by the National Association of Real Estate Boards, it is independent of it. It also acts as technical consultant to the National Association of Home Builders on land development. From its inception the approach has been toward the practical and realistic application of sound principles developed through the actual experience of outstanding men in the urban development field, and in making their experience available. In 1944, in furtherance of this objective, Hugh Potter, nationally known developer of River Oaks, Houston, Texas, one of the founders and then President of the Institute, was instrumental in organizing the Community Builders' Council. It is composed of a small group of men, geographically distributed throughout the United States and Canada, who were selected for their outstanding experience in and contribution to the field of community development.

The objective of this group was, and continues to be, the provision of a much needed medium whereby the practices and knowledge of community builders could be exchanged, analyzed, and evaluated in the light of long and intimate experience, and this combined experience made available to men entering the community building and land development field as well as those now in it.

These men have given unstintingly of their time, and traveled long distances at their own expense in pursuing this objective. In numerous three to four-day sessions of intensive work which have taken place to date under the able chairmanship of J. C. Nichols, developer of the famous Country Club District, Kansas City, the Council has emphasized the practical and realistic aspects of community development against the background of sound city and community planning principles.

The Handbook is the result of this combined knowledge of the Council members, edited by men with wide experience in city and community planning. Seward H. Mott, Editor, and Executive Director of U. L. I., is nationally known as a consultant in land planning and is former Director of the Land Planning Division of the Federal Housing Administration. Max S. Wehrly, Associate Editor, was formerly the City Planner of the National

Capital Park and Planning Commission of Washington, D. C. and has done much consulting work in planning, zoning, and subdivision regulations. Both men are the authors of numerous articles on the subject of city and community planning. I feel, therefore, that the Handbook sets forth the best thought in community development gleaned from this combined effort.

The Council members all believe strongly that too little thought and study has heretofore been given to community building, particularly the creation of enduring values of neighborhoods, the encouragement of home ownership, and the promotion of sound investment in land development for homes and community shopping centers. They believe that stable, attractive, and self-supporting home communities can be built for a wide range of incomes by private initiative without governmental paternalistic help.

It has not been fully recognized that many shopping centers have not been profitable ventures, often earning little or no returns on the investment. It has also not been realized that the great instability and rapid shifts in the character and make-up of our urban areas have created a tremendous deficit in terms of obsolescence, loss of taxable values, and spread of decadence and blight estimated at several billion dollars annually. The Council's answer to this problem is not, as advocated by some, to continue to tear down and rebuild every 25 to 35 years, but rather to build enduring values. To do this we must think in terms of generations, not decades.

The ultra-modernist and the seeker for radical, unorthodox, or socialized departures in this field will not find them here. What he will find will be considered recommendations of methods and procedures which have stood the test of sound land planning and engineering design, of the financial risks involved, and, most important, ideas which have the acceptance of the American home-buying public which is traditionally moderate in its selection of a home. This is usually the family's largest life investment, and the Council feels it is not the place for irresponsible experimentation. This book is intended rather to pass on to those younger men now in the field or about to enter it, the most modern practices of progressive men who have tried and proved the suggestions set forth as sound through years of actual application.

The Council feels strongly that it is only through this approach that the maximum benefits are to be realized: to the developer in producing a sound and financially successful project; to the resident of the community in enhanced living environment and amenities; and to the community as a whole in the creation of a well designed physical development and enduring taxable income upon which it must depend for its continued welfare.

We ask everyone who reads this Handbook to send any comments or suggestions they may have to Seward H. Mott, Executive Director of the Urban Land Institute, and we would welcome their joining with us in carrying on further research and practical studies in community planning. The Council is continuing its work, including field studies of outstanding developments throughout the country, with the view to adding future supplements to the Handbook. It is also planned to continue and expand the program of Council sessions and open forums. Toward this end the Council has recently been opened to additional land developers, community builders, and others operating in the field of land development. The original Council which prepared this volume will continue as the Executive and Research Committee of this larger group.

A group similar to the Community Builders' Council known as the Central Business District Council was organized in 1945 to study the central areas of our cities. This Council is headed by A. J. Stewart, Vice President of the Citizens Fidelity Bank and Trust Company of Louisville, and is composed of a group of equally distinguished men in the fields of downtown real estate, commerce, banking and property investment.

NEWTON C. FARR, *President,*
Urban Land Institute.

Chicago, Illinois,
September 4, 1947.

"*A home is not a detached unit but a part of a neighborhood, which in turn is part of a town; and the good quality of the home usually depends at least as much on its surroundings as on its design and construction. Hence the vital importance of ground planning and control of the development of neighborhoods.*" —THOMAS ADAMS.

Table of Contents

PART I

PRELIMINARY STEPS IN COMMUNITY DEVELOPMENT

PART II

PLANNING THE DEVELOPMENT

List of Illustrations

PLATES

FIGURES

TABLES

THE
COMMUNITY BUILDERS
HANDBOOK

PART I

Preliminary Steps in Community Development

"In our early 'single residential' developments we overestimated our market and acquired too much land—creating too large a carrying load in interest, taxes, and maintenance. I strongly recommend that every developer make a careful market analysis of the needs of his community before he develops a new area for sale." J. C. NICHOLS.

In order to follow this advice, the following procedures and sources of information are outlined for ready reference by the developer.

A. MARKET ANALYSIS.

1. Sources of Information.

Before acquiring land for a development, a careful analysis of the local market should be made. This can be based upon the following sources of information:

(a) The local city planning commission, zoning board, and other local agencies having to do with land development and erection of buildings.

(b) 16th Census—U. S. Census State Bulletins—1940. These bulletins cover each state and the principal cities therein. It would be well for the developer to check one or more of the following:

Population

(1) FIRST SERIES—Number of Inhabitants.
(2) SECOND SERIES—Characteristics of the Population.
(3) THIRD SERIES—The Labor Force: Occupation, Industry, Employment and Income.
(4) FOURTH SERIES—Characteristics by Age, Marital Status, Relationship, Education and Citizenship.
(5) POPULATION AND HOUSING—Statistics for Census Tracts.

Housing

(6) FIRST SERIES—Data for Small Areas.
(7) SUPPLEMENT TO FIRST SERIES—Block Statistics.
(8) SECOND SERIES—General Characteristics.
(9) THIRD SERIES—Characteristics by Monthly Rent or Value.
(10) FOURTH SERIES—Mortgages on Owner-Occupied Non-Farm Homes.

1

(11) Service Establishments.
(12) Retail Trade—Census of Business, 1939.
(13) Wholesale Trade—Census of Business, 1939.
(14) Manufactures—1939.

The above bulletins can be obtained free of charge by writing to the Division of Information of Publications, U. S. Census, Washington 25, D. C. It should be recognized that the Census data is now over seven years old and that the war has brought about abrupt changes in many areas. Thus current data, in some instances, if it were available might be radically different from that of 1940. However, most of the information can be used as a check against current estimates which can then be determined with reasonable accuracy from personal knowledge and from other sources such as those listed below.

(c) Current population estimates secured from local utility companies, such as the telephone, electric, gas and transit companies, The Bureau of Employment Security, Federal Security Agency, and the U. S. Census.

(d) U. S. Dept. of Labor—Bureau of Labor Statistics, Employment and Occupational Outlook Branch. Industrial Area Studies and Industrial Area Statistics Summaries.

(e) Studies by local manufacturers on estimates of employment trends.

(f) Real Property Inventories. Although these were made in 1934-36, they may be useful in showing trends and can be compared within reasonable limits with the 1940 Census housing data. A large number of cities were covered in this inventory and these may be obtained from the Publications Unit, Bureau of Foreign and Domestic Commerce, Washington, D. C.

(g) Many local Boards of Trade and Chambers of Commerce maintain a research and statistical service on the business, industrial, and building outlook.

2. Data to be Included.

The market analysis should include the following data and considerations:

(a) *Population Changes*. Will there be an increase or decrease; at what rate; will the community hold its own? Do not make the error of relying on past trends alone; factors responsible for past growth may have disappeared. Population in many cities, particularly in the northeast, has become static or is declining. This apparent trend should, however, be checked against suburban trends which may show substantial population increases. The metropolitan area should be the unit for analysis. Rate and direction of growth and decentralization trends will influence size and location of the project and speed of development.

In this connection it is interesting to note the growth trends in both the cities and the nation as a whole. In 1880, the date of birth of the Council's Chairman, the population of the country numbered about 50 million persons of whom only 14 million or 28 percent lived in urban places. Twenty years later these figures had increased to 76 million for the nation of which 30 million or 40 percent were urban residents. In 1946 the population stood at 137 million with 60 percent in the urban areas.[1] During this entire period the size of the family decreased, being about 5 persons for the nation in 1880; 4.6 in 1940; and 3.6 in 1946, with the urban figure somewhat lower. It should be emphasized that this was a period of extremely rapid growth, both for nation and city, which is not likely to be repeated. Population authorities look forward to a continuing decline in the rate of growth which may reach a near static condition around 1980. However, it is expected that the upward trend in the percentage of urban population will continue to a point in the vicinity of perhaps three-quarters of our total population. In general, this national picture is and will continue to be reflected in the local areas within which the developer is working.

In what areas are population changes likely to take place? Planning commissions usually have maps showing population trends. Location of industry and transportation facilities will give indications. Building permit spot maps will reveal the active areas, extent and direction of urban development.

(b) *Occupations.* What are the occupations of the potential buyers or renters and numbers of each?

(c) *Incomes.* What are the probable incomes of families within the area? Compare these with estimates of income needed to maintain families at different standards of living. Estimate numbers who can afford homes in various price ranges and compare with the present supply and probable demand for a period of several years ahead. Also, do not overlook the age grouping, sex and marital status of the community, and the declining size

---

[1] An additional 4 million were in the armed services on this date.

of families, as this will reflect the future housing demand and types of businesses required.

(d) *Housing Inventory.* What housing accommodations are now available? A survey of dwelling units should cover such information as the dwelling type, age, condition and size, vacancy, and rental value. Such a survey should consider the existing substandard housing and any plans for its demolition or rehabilitation.

(e) *Construction Costs.* At what price ranges can new housing be absorbed?

(f) *Tax Rates and Assessments.* Analysis of the market should also include a comparison of tax rates and assessments in adjacent competing communities in comparison with the public services rendered. Do not overlook the standards of school instruction as this will affect demand by families with children.

(g) The planning commission, zoning boards, adjoining county officials, and the local FHA office can often furnish data in the form of maps, charts and future plans which will help to evaluate quickly any contemplated site with relation to competing sites and to the entire urban area.

B. TECHNICAL PLANNING SERVICE.

Before selecting and planning a site, time and money will be saved by obtaining technical services in the following fields. Several of these services may occasionally be offered by one individual or by an "office" where several individuals give complete services. No part of a development can be considered separately, but the following designate normally accepted fields of technical knowledge.

1. Land Planning, Site Planning and Landscape Architecture.

Land and site planning involves questions of site location and the determination and allocation of the specific uses of land, including means of access and communication, topography, vehicular and pedestrian traffic, open spaces and areas for residential, commercial and industrial uses, all coordinated to produce a unified development which can be built economically, operated efficiently and maintained with normal expense. Landscape architecture deals more specifically with the design and treatment of ground forms and plant materials, detailed relationships of buildings to site, design of open spaces around buildings, and of recreation and other use areas.

4

2. Engineering.

Engineering includes the kind of service needed to establish precise location of streets, lot and building lines, etc., and to furnish topographic maps, detailed data and working drawings as may be needed for grades, earthwork, street improvements, storm water drainage, sanitary sewers, water supply and other public utilities. Figure 1 indicates the type of engineering data usually required on a subdivision plat of record.

3. Architecture.

Architecture involves the planning, design, and construction of buildings and other structures.

The developer will find that it pays to get the best technical services available. Competent, widely experienced land planning engineers and architects can through skillful treatment greatly increase property values, decrease construction and maintenance costs, and add tremendously to the appeal and marketability of any development. The returns from the services of good technicians may amount to many times their cost. Don't try to save pennies here. Pay a fair fee, you will make money on it. However, the developer must finally weigh and analyze all studies and recommendations as to their practicabilities. Many developments in the United States have been too extravagantly planned and have ended in financial failure. In the last analysis the vital question is "Will it pay?" This cannot be left to the final decision of the planner or architect.

C. SELECTION OF SUBDIVISION SITE.

1. Accessibility and Transportation.

Poor location is one of the most common causes for the failure of developments. Transportation facilities to places of work, central business areas, schools, churches, and recreation are primary considerations. The following may be used as rules of thumb, particularly for low cost developments. See also Figure 2 showing maximum distances to employment and other facilities.

(a) *Walking Distances.* (Good) When the site is within walking distance of places of employment. (Poor) When the site lacks public transit and is over one mile walking distance from places of employment.

5

Figure 1.

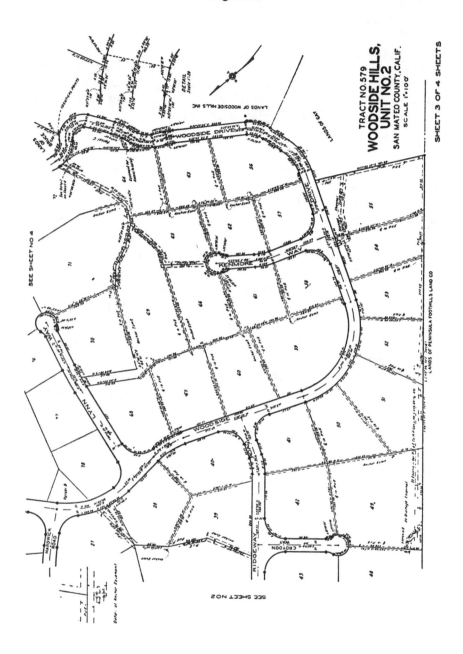

Plat showing needed survey data for record plat.

(b) *Transportation.* (Good) When time of travel is less than 30 minutes. Where there is good transportation, industrial workers do not always choose to live too close to their work. Many do not wish to associate altogether with the people with whom they work all day. (Fair) When travel time is over 30 minutes but not more than 45 minutes. (Poor) When travel time is over 45 minutes, except in a few of the larger cities where one hour is not considered excessive.

It should be emphasized that except in the highest priced developments, complete reliance on the private automobile for transportation to and from places of employment and shopping is not advisable. Proximity to good mass transit facilities will continue to be of distinct importance.

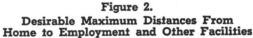

Figure 2.
Desirable Maximum Distances From
Home to Employment and Other Facilities

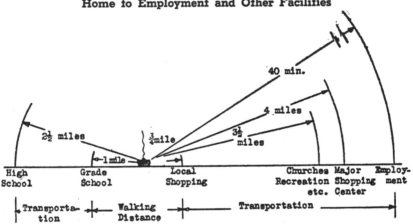

Desirable maximum distances to employment and other facilities within which it is felt feasible or safe to build residential developments. The distance to a high school in some localities may be unimportant because of school bus transportation.

Source: Opinion Surveys of developers and others by the Urban Land Institute, Technical Bulletin No. 3.

2. Location and Approaches.

Of utmost importance to the success of the development is its location within the urban area, the manner in which the major thoroughfare routes approach it, and the character of existing and future development along these routes.

A "good address" for medium to high priced projects is especially important. Such projects should preferably be on the "right side" of town. Fighting long established adverse trends

Figure 3.
Shifts in Location of Fashionable Residential Areas
in Six American Cities
1900-1936

Fashionable residential areas, indicated by solid black, show the same general directional movement outward from the center over a period of years.

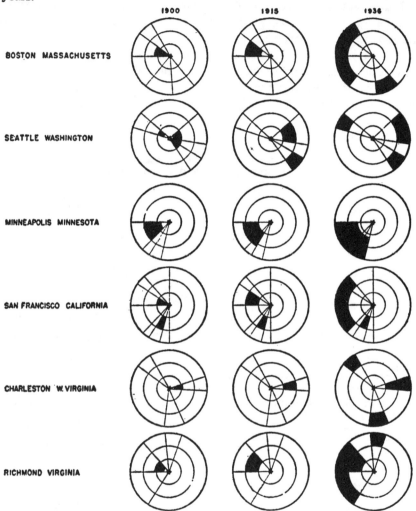

Source: Federal Housing Administration, Division of Economics & Statistics.

may prove difficult and expensive. In low cost projects, land costs, convenience to work, schools, and shopping, are frequently more important factors than a "good address".

Factors which should be considered in the selection of any site include the following:

8

Figure 4.

Growth of Residential Areas
Chicago 1857-1930

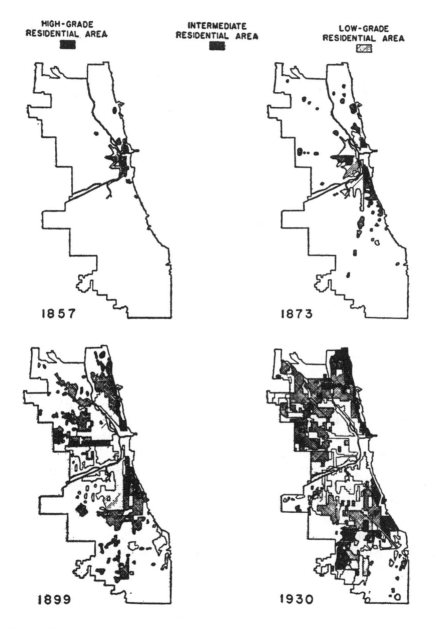

HIGH-GRADE RESIDENTIAL AREA

INTERMEDIATE RESIDENTIAL AREA

LOW-GRADE RESIDENTIAL AREA

1857

1873

1899

1930

Source: Hoyt, Homer, *"One Hundred Years of Land Values in Chicago,"* (Chicago, University of Chicago Press, 1933) p. 319

(a) Trends in past city growth should be carefully studied to determine the direction in which high, medium and low cost developments have tended to move. It is very difficult to reverse major directional trends. High value development, subject to local factors, will usually continue to move outward from the central district in radial or segmental patterns. Prestige is added to a project if located in the "proper" section of the urban area. Figures 3 and 4 will serve to illustrate the movement of fashionable residential areas in seven American cities. Exceptions to this rule will of course be found.

(b) If access to the site is available only over congested routes, or through depreciated commercial, industrial, or residential areas, it will probably be wise not to consider it for a high class development and to abandon the site in favor of one with more favorable approach routes. It may, however, be possible in some instances to acquire additional land or obtain rights-of-way which will permit an entirely new or improved approach, at least to the general vicinity of the development. Two examples may be cited:

In Shaker Heights, one of the largest fine residential developments in the country located near Cleveland, Ohio, the developers purchased the Nickel Plate Railroad right-of-way in order to secure a new and direct approach to the development. This cost millions of dollars and is of course an unusual situation which would rarely be duplicated.

In Upper Arlington, Columbus, Ohio, a 3,000 acre residential development, a strip of land four miles long was acquired to provide a quick and pleasing approach to the central district of the city. In both cases the acquisition of a good approach was a major factor in making the development possible.

There is considerable evidence to indicate that the provision of urban expressways, more accurately called freeways because of their limited access features, will tend to bring about more outlying residential development. Limited access highways of this type provide both for ease in reaching the central city area and for rapid movement of traffic to outlying points.

Regarding the entrance to the development itself, J. C. Nichols makes the following observation based on experience in the

Plate I. Simple but effective entrance treatment.
"HILLSDALE," San Mateo, California.
David D. Bohannon Organization.

Country Club District: "Too much money can be spent in building elaborate gateways and entrances. These gateways frequently deter the sales of lots immediately adjoining. Such entrance features should be modest and not too conspicuous except in very unusual locations. They should blend into their particular surroundings." (See Plate I.)

3. Size of Development.

The size of the tract that can be handled financially must be carefully considered before acreage is purchased. Because of taxes and high carrying charges, it is not practical to carry too much acreage at any one time. The average subdivision in the United States is approximately 35 acres, but, generally, larger areas should be developed at one time, and, if possible, contiguous holdings of several hundred acres be controlled.

Preliminary sketch plans can be quickly worked out for various proposed subdivision sites which will indicate the approximate number of lot units after deducting streets, parks, and waste areas. Such approximations should then be related to the ability of the developer to sell over a period of time and to carry the costs of land purchase and development. Many developers have "gone broke" trying to carry too much acreage. Compound interest must always be figured on unsold land and improvements.

Where possible, according to Maurice Read of Berkeley, future expansion should be available through long-time options on adjoining areas.

4. Land Cost.

The proposed selling or rental price of the dwelling units, based on careful analysis of the market, should determine the price that can be paid for the land, and not the reverse. According to Cyrus Willmore of St. Louis, an improved lot for houses to sell under $10,000 can normally be figured at about 15 per cent of the total house cost and may gradually be raised to as high as 25 per cent for homes costing $25,000 or over. See Tables 1 to 3 showing valuation of improved land compared with property valuations. Deducting the estimated cost of improvements, profit, overhead, and carrying charges should give the amount which can be paid for the raw lot.

5. Physical Characteristics of the Site.

(a) *Topography and Shape of Site.* Moderately sloping sites are preferable to either steep or very level land. As a rule it has

Table 1.

Relation Between Cost of Lot and of House For Typical Medium Cost Houses

City	Average Per Cent Cost of Lot of Cost of House and Lot	Average Size of Lot
500,000 and over	20.2	42 x 127*
300,000 to 500,000	17.5	49 x 133*
100,000 to 300,000	18.1	51 x 123
50,000 to 100,000	17.7	50 x 124
Under 50,000	18.7	46 x 124*

From Table XIII *"Neighborhoods of Small Homes"* by Whitten and Adams, Harvard City Planning Series, Vol. III, 1931.

Table 2.

Relation Between Cost of Lot and of House For Typical Low-Cost House

City	Average Per Cent Lot Value of Sale Price of House and Lot	Average Size of Lot
500,000 and over	24.1	41 x 102*
300,000 to 500,000	18.5	45 x 115*
100,000 to 300,000	18.6	48 x 131*

From Table XIV *"Neighborhoods of Small Homes"* by Whitten & Adams, Harvard City Planning Series, Vol. III, 1931.

* The Council does not recommend lots as narrow as these.

Table 3.

Valuation of Improved Land Compared With Property Valuation

Property Valuation Classes	IN METROPOLITAN DISTRICTS	
	Average Land Valuation in Dollars	Land As a Per Cent of Property
$4,000 — $4,999	553	12.5
5,000 — 5,999	654	12.1
6,000 — 6,999	848	13.5
7,000 — 7,999	1078	14.7
8,000 — 9,999	1325	15.4
10,000 — 11,999	1739	16.4
12,000 — 14,999	2326	18.0
15,000 — and over	3264	18.7
All Classes: 1940	698	13.1
1939	770	13.9
1938	848	14.7
1937	1011	15.9

Source: Federal Housing Administration, 7th Annual Report, 1940. (Based on 1940 costs.)

Present costs will affect these ratios, with trends toward a higher percentage for improved lots.

been found that improvement costs rise sharply on slopes of over 8 to 10 per cent. Heavy grading creates settlement and erosion problems. Although the original unit cost of rough broken land may be less, it will frequently be found to cost so much more to grade and make useable that the final improved lot costs will be higher than if more expensive but more level land were purchased. Hugh Prather states that for higher priced properties where lots are large, broken topography and wooded areas may work out very well, but for low cost homes where lot costs must be held to a minimum, cleared, gently rolling and well drained land is by far the best. Very flat land presents numerous problems in sewerage and storm drainage that may raise improvement costs to a very high figure.

The shape of the subdivision site should be compact. Irregular boundaries and the presence of utility or railway easements may result in waste areas and uneconomical street and lot layouts.[1]

(b) *Drainage and Subgrade.* A site should have good natural surface drainage. Watch out for marsh or swamp areas or wet pockets which must be drained, frequently at prohibitive cost. Clay-loam, sand, gravel or other porous material afford good soil drainage and economical construction. Sites which have served as dumps or have otherwise been filled, and sites which have underlying rock close to the surface or high ground water, should be avoided. Test holes should be dug in various parts of the property and conditions carefully noted.[2]

(c) *Tree Growth.* Scattered existing trees are desirable, but if low cost houses are contemplated, heavily wooded, brushy or stony sites requiring extensive clearing should be avoided. Clearing of such land frequently runs to $100 or more per lot, which might be greater than its raw land value.

6. Utility Services.

No factor in site selection is more important than the availability of water, sanitary and storm sewers, electricity, gas, and public transportation. Not only should the lines for these services be at or near the site, but they should also be of adequate

---

[1] U. S. Geological Survey quadrangle sheets, or in certain localities, more recent maps prepared by the War Department, will be of value in evaluating the general location and topographic character of the site. These may be obtained from the U. S. Geological Survey, Dept. of Interior, Washington, D. C. and from the Commanding Officer, Army Map Service, 6500 Brooks Lane, Washington, D. C. for 10 cents per sheet.

[2] See A of Part II, Site Information For Planning.

15

capacity to carry the increased load of the new development and future development of the surrounding tributary area. Check this carefully with your city and county departments and utility companies.

(a) *Water.* Public water supply mains at or near the site are most desirable. Individual wells give water that may vary in quantity and quality, and individual pumps require frequent inspection and maintenance. In some areas small community water companies have been formed by developers. They are usually controlled by state utility commissions or health departments and are much superior to individual wells, but they also add to the problem of development, and are much less desirable than a public water supply. Cooperative water companies in which the property owners are members generally have not proved successful and are not recommended.

Adjacent water mains should be checked for quantity and pressure to assure normal supply that is sufficient for present and future fire protection.

(b) *Sewerage.* A public sanitary sewer system that may service the site is also most desirable. Individual septic tanks and cesspools for sewage disposal are rarely completely satisfactory. As a rule the cost of a properly constructed and maintained septic tank and disposal field is greater than the proportionate cost of public sewers. It has also been found that in many areas there is sales resistance to the septic tank. A community sewer system installed by the developer with a monthly rental charge is superior to individual septic tanks and has proved successful in many parts of the country. Provision should be made for its continued operation. (See also page 77.)

With public sewers of adequate size adjacent to the site, invert elevations should be carefully checked by the site planner or engineer with all parts of the site to determine whether or not they can be used. Sites lower than the adjacent sewerage system will involve pumping problems requiring future fixed maintenance charges.

(c) *Storm Water.* Surface drainage is usually taken care of by a sewerage system separate from the sanitary sewers. It is desirable that either existing storm sewers of sufficient size be available or that there exist streams or valleys into which storm drainage can be discharged. You can not cut off natural drainage of adjacent land, and you may not be able to dump excessively accumulated water on your neighbor or even in any stream or public drain without definite and written permission from the owner or the public authority. Do not overlook this point and be sure to obtain the necessary clearances. Don't overlook the greatly increased run-off of water as an area becomes fully developed, including the entire watershed.

(d) *Electricity and Gas.* These services are normally supplied by private utility companies at their own expense. It is necessary that electricity be available at the site for light and power, also for cooking and heating water in the event that gas is not available. In choosing a site, the location and capacity of all distribution lines in the vicinity should be indicated on study maps. At the start of a residential development, it is common practice for the private utility company to charge the developer for the cost of main extensions and then to refund as customers are added.

(e) *Utility Costs.* Costs of installing underground utilities have increased greatly in recent years. The requirement that the developer bear the full burden of these costs results in a substantial increase in the initial cost of the property to the purchaser. The Council strongly recommends that where municipalities obtain revenue from water service or through sewer fees, they should bear the cost of such installations from the revenue so derived. This would substantially lower the initial cost to the developer and purchaser alike. Cities now charging such installation costs to the developer, or which, in addition, assess the home owner, are urged to change their practice.

Regarding the extent to which utilities should be installed at any one time by the developer, John Mowbray of Baltimore warns: "Don't make the mistake of installing street improvements and utilities on too much land in advance of sales. This greatly increases the carrying load, tends to create shop-worn property, and takes away interest, zeal and sales value in opening new areas. Buyers like new offerings."

7. Site Environment.

(a) *Land Use.* The site should be reasonably free from the influence of nearby undesirable land uses. If the area is zoned, consult the zoning map and regulations.

Undesirable surroundings such as railroad tracks, cemeteries, poorly subdivided and cheap developments, or poor commercial or industrial uses must be guarded against. Physical buffers such as parks, golf courses, river valleys and certain types of institutional properties may minimize such bad effects. Buffers of plantings and screen walls can be created, but such corrective measures must be taken into account in the land cost. Judson Bradway of Detroit emphasizes that land which can be bought cheaply because of poor surroundings is seldom a bargain.

(b) *Traffic Streets.* Freedom of the site from the adverse effects of through traffic is highly important. Proximity of heavy

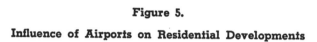

Figure 5.

Influence of Airports on Residential Developments

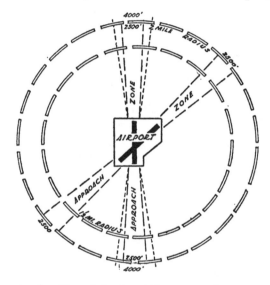

1. Major airports should not be located nearer than two miles from a residential area.
2. Areas in approach zones and within two miles of end of major airstrips are definitely objectionable to residential developments.
3. Airparks for small planes should not be located nearer than 1½ miles from residential developments.
4. Normal approach at 30:1 glide angle plane elevation at two miles is 352 feet.
5. Instrument approach at 40:1 glide angle plane elevation at two miles is 264 feet.
6. Width of approach zones at the two-mile radius is 2500 feet for contact flying and 4000 feet for instrument flying. Planes do not always stay within these approach zones.

Source: Opinion Surveys of developers and others by the Urban Land Institute, based on operating conditions. Technical Bulletin No. 3.

traffic streets can be as detrimental as cheap developments or commercial and industrial uses. Where possible, sites split by existing or potential major thoroughfares should be avoided. Check with your planning commission and highway department on this matter, and, if possible, endeavor to have proposed thoroughfares relocated along the periphery of the community. Any additional land dedicated to the municipality or county to achieve this end may pay big dividends. To avoid interference with sleep and outdoor living, larger, deeper lots on heavily travelled thoroughfares are desirable.

(c) *Dampness, Smoke, and Views.* A site should be free from smoke and offensive odors. The direction of prevailing winds and of periodic storms and fog is important in many areas. Good views and a pleasing outlook, according to Hugh Russell of Seattle, are great assets and should be carefully preserved.

(d) *Flooding.* Check all low sites for likelihood of present and future flooding. If the site contains sufficient buildable area above flood height, the lower land may be reserved for park and play areas. Frequently land subject to flood can be filled above flood dangers with excess excavation. However, don't underestimate the increased run-off which results as an entire watershed is developed.

(e) *Fire Hazard.* Proximity to large tanks for the storage of gas, oil, and other inflammable materials should be avoided.

(f) *Airports.* Property for residential purposes may be adversely affected in varying degrees within two miles of any commercial airport. The glide angle for take-off and landing of transport planes is small, and at normal 30 or 40 to one glide ratios, a plane is only 260 to 350 feet above ground level at a distance of two miles from an airport runway. The noise, vibration, and hazard—psychological as well as real—are definitely objectionable to residential areas at lesser distances. Airparks for small private planes adversely affect property within 1½ miles. See Fig. 5 and Table 4 which show the adverse influence of airports on residential developments.[1]

---

[1] A number of the Council found that large airports within 2½ miles have proven objectionable to residents in the area. Cyrus Crane Willmore, St. Louis, has stated that small airports would be more objectionable than large ones because of the aimless flying of small planes. J. C. Nichols, Kansas City, feels that we have greatly overrated the use of airports. Generally the Community Builders' Council members are opposed to having airports or "airparks" located near their developments, under present conditions.

Table 4.
Estimated Effect of Airports on Land Values
Detroit, Michigan

Site		0 TO ½ MILE ZONE SURROUNDING SITE				½ TO 1 MILE ZONE SURROUNDING SITE				TOTAL LOSSES	
	Items	Present Value	Appraiser's % Loss in Value	Appraiser's Loss in Value	Items	Present Value	Appraiser's % Loss	Appraiser's Loss in Value	Appraiser's Total Loss in Value	Consultants' Estimated Total Loss
SITE No. 1	2 Farm Bldgs.	6,500			1 Farm Bldg.	3,000				
	2105 Residential Bldgs.	5,442,100	27.5*	1,498,500	4010 Residential Bldgs.	18,232,500	18.6	3,396,600		
	1200 Acres—Subdivisions	4,160,000	74.4	3,096,800	2960 Acres—Subdivisions	7,002,000	71.0	4,970,500		
	1680 Acres—Farm Land	480,000			1200 Acres—Farm Land	370,000				
	Totals	$10,088,600		$4,595,300	Totals	$25,607,500		$8,367,100	$12,962,400	$5,739,400
SITE No. 2	17 Farm Bldgs.	68,500			22 Farm Bldgs.	89,500				
	862 Residential Bldgs.	3,651,100	34.1	1,243,800	1088 Residential Bldgs.	4,659,900	18.9	879,400		
	1790 Acres—Subdivisions	2,300,000	92.7	2,131,200	2250 Acres—Subdivisions	2,169,000	89.3	1,937,400		
	1410 Acres—Farm Land	429,000			2230 Acres—Farm Land	821,000				
	Totals	$6,448,600		$3,375,000	Totals	$7,739,400		$2,816,800	$6,191,800	$2,703,200
SITE No. 3	21 Farm Bldgs.	85,400			27 Farm Bldgs.	111,100				
	978 Residential Bldgs.	3,871,700	23.3	903,300	1009 Residential Bldgs.	3,036,700	20.7	629,300		
	2220 Acres—Subdivisions	1,902,000	77.2	1,468,600	2400 Acres—Subdivisions	2,326,000	89.5	2,081,300		
	1060 Acres—Farm Land	306,000			2080 Acres—Farm Land	620,000				
	Totals	$6,165,100		$2,372,400	Totals	$6,093,800		$2,710,600	$5,083,000	$2,200,600
SITE No. 4	26 Farm Bldgs.	94,100			23 Farm Bldgs.	94,700				
	687 Residential Bldgs.	2,302,800	32.3	742,500	1036 Residential Bldgs.	3,462,000	14.7	508,900		
	1204 Acres—Subdivisions	935,300	87.0	813,300	1860 Acres—Subdivisions	1,663,000	86.9	1,449,000		
	1996 Acres—Farm Land	450,800			2620 Acres—Farm Land	570,000				
	Totals	$3,783,000		$1,555,800	Totals	$5,794,700		$1,957,900	$3,513,700	$1,539,400

* 0% Loss estimated for negro housing development.
Percentage excluding negro housing development 44.2%.

From report prepared by the associate firms of Horner and Shifrin and Smith, Hinchman and Grylls, Inc. for the Detroit Metropolitan Aviation Planning Authority, July 1945.
(See report notes, page 21.)

Although the experience of the Council members with airports has been definitely unfavorable, it is recognized that future improvements in aircraft, landing facilities and operational regulations may reduce one or more of their objectionable features. With this in mind several aviation organizations were requested to comment on future possibilities in this respect.

Lowell H. Swenson, Executive Vice President of the National Aeronautic Association, says in part: "It is recognized by the more progressive segments of aviation, that it will be impossible to obtain popular acceptance for more airports until the use to

---

Notes on Table 4.

"In this Table there are shown the present estimated values of lands and improvements surrounding each of the airport sites as accumulated by the staff of the Consultants. This information is shown under the Columns headed 'Present Value.' The figures in the Columns headed 'Appraisers' Loss in Value' have been worked out in detail on the basis of percentage of loss for various classes of property, at various distances from the airport boundary, as set out in a letter of July 9th from Roy Wenzlick & Co., Economists and Appraisers of New York and St. Louis, a copy of which has been filed with the Authority.

"The Columns headed 'Appraiser Percentage Loss' contain average percentages worked out by the Consultants from the relation to the Columns on each side.

"The figures shown under 'Appraiser Loss in Value' are responsive to the advice contained in the Wenzlick letter. They may be taken as the loss expected by these Counselors to result from the operation of a Major Airport.

"The Consultants understand that this estimate of loss is based on the Counselors' study of conditions at existing airports, and is related to the present type of transport planes and their operation.

"On this basis the loss shown may be taken as that which would occur around a new Major Airport with a dense traffic of planes of the present type.

"The Consultants are of the opinion that the aircraft construction industry will greatly reduce such nuisance factors in connection with the new planes which are to be expected hereafter. This would be particularly true as turbine and jet propulsion comes into the picture. Accepting the appraisers' opinion of the loss which might occur during the early period of airport operation, the Consultants conclude, however, that much of this should be recovered as improved types of planes come into use. They have recognized the situation and have adopted, on the basis of long range planning, an ultimate smaller figure of loss in value shown in the last Column."

EDITORS' NOTE.—The Consultants appeared to be over-optimistic. Two years after the report there is no indication that plane improvements will decrease their objectionable features in any great degree.

which the fields are put no longer is considered a hazard or nuisance to the surrounding area, and until the fields themselves are more attractive. In short, airports must be 'better neighbors'.

"Unfortunately, this concept has come too late to be applied to many existing airports. It is improbable that an area would be desirable for residential development when located adjacent to a field used for passenger or cargo service, charter flying, instruction, repair or maintenance.

"Residential developers will, therefore, want to know if it would be wise to plan for proximity to the true 'airpark' of the future.

" 'Airparks' should be foreseen as exclusively for small privately owned aircraft, and would be roughly comparable to the present provision for group parking or garaging automobiles. Landing areas would be of sod. There would be individual hangars for the planes conforming to the architecture of the adjacent development, with the airpark similarly landscaped. There would be no business activities, no repair bases, fuel services, or the like. The field would be for the use of personal owners, taking off from, or returning to, the field nearest their homes. The character of operations from the field would be controlled just as the type of traffic on parkways is regulated.

"This type of field, from a scenic standpoint, undoubtedly would be acceptable to prospective buyers of homes in the development. It would have to be unobjectionable in other respects. Objections to residing near an airport generally take three forms: noise, danger, and property depreciation. The NAA has made a close study of these objections. Its considered opinion is that noise is the crux of the matter.

"Airplanes do make noise. It is an unfamiliar type of noise, is intermittent, and annoying probably to the bulk of people. This is being recognized increasingly by those responsible for designing and building aircraft. Personal aircraft now are quieter than those built immediately after the war. Those built next year will be more quiet. How long it will be before the noise level is reduced to below the nuisance point is problematical, but there is reason to believe it will be within five years.

"Regulations have been proposed prohibiting all flying over built-up areas except that necessary to leave or land at airports, strictly enforced by local officials and self-policed by the pilots, sales and service operators, and airport managers, as a temporary solution to the airplane noise nuisance during the period in which the quiet airplane is being evolved. All of this indicates that quieter airplanes are far beyond the stage of mere talk. They will be in existence within a few years. That should have some implication for community builders in their consideration of the extent to which plans should provide for home owners who want to and can afford to fly."

Joseph T. Gueting, Manager of the Personal Aircraft Council, A. I. A. presents the position of the Aircraft Industries Association as follows: "It is the considered opinion of the aircraft manufacturing industry, particularly that section devoted to the production of personal aircraft, that any planning for the future development of new residential areas must necessarily include provision of suitable aircraft landing facilities immediately adjacent to such new areas. It should be significant that there now are over 90,000 individually owned and operated personal aircraft in this country. This total will probably reach 100,000 by the end of 1947.

"An airpark can no longer be classed as a luxury; it is as much a necessity as the railroad depot and the highway that serve to link the community to the nation. Many communities today are faced with the necessity of making great physical changes due to the fact that years ago, when the automobile was in the same stage of development as the airplane is today, proper foresight was not exercised in the geographical layout of residential and business areas."

Taking a somewhat broader view of the problem, George W. Burgess, Deputy Administrator of the Civil Aeronautics Administration, says: "The CAA has been aware of the importance of integrating airports it helps build into the community plan, and making them real assets to the community.

"The CAA has prepared its National Airport Plan with great care, with the interests of the entire community in mind. In metropolitan areas, it is required that a master plan be submitted, showing all the proposed airports of various types—private and transport—and how they fit into the general land use scheme. This plan is reviewed to make sure airports are located to best serve potential flyers and the community generally. This can be accomplished by selecting a site where the runway approaches will be over the least populated areas, or by placing the airport in a section that is relatively undeveloped but easily accessible by public means and an express highway. Where no general land use scheme has been adopted, CAA still reviews the proposed site with the long-range interest of the community as criterion.

"These standards will apply to more than 4,000 airport projects which will be undertaken during the Federal Aid program. Projects which private enterprise may launch during the same period inevitably will be spurred to match these standards. CAA planning advice is available to them.

"Another attack on this problem is the work done on the development of quieter airplanes. The National Advisory Committee on Aeronautics has done extensive research on reducing propeller as well as exhaust noise. This research work is now being brought to a point of practical application by the Aeronautical Research Foundation.

"Quieting the airplane is something that can be expected— in the meantime much can be done by enforcing its thoughtful and proper use. Show-off or needless low flying accounts for most of the complaints directed against the aircraft. The CAA has worked out a cooperative program with state and local law enforcement officials designed to curb this kind of flying, with salutary effects.

"In short, residential developers may be assured that the aviation fraternity fully appreciates the importance of developing the goodwill of the public and the home owner."

These statements appear to disregard or minimize certain rather vital aspects of the airport problem from the standpoint of the community builder. The builder, however, cannot afford to do this. The success or failure of any given development may depend upon estimating carefully and correctly these and other factors which affect his project, both at present and in the future. For instance, it is seriously questioned if even a private airpark could continue to operate successfully without providing fuel and minor repair services sufficient to insure the minimum of safety in the air. Experience with the automobile has shown clearly that where a demand develops these facilities are eventually provided, often to the detriment of adjacent residential property.

Low flying, hovering and maneuvering of aircraft over private property can be fully as objectionable as noise. This form of nuisance is widespread today and would not be remedied by noise reduction. A well designed, modern community plan while making provisions for the automobile offers at the same time the maximum discouragement to automobile traffic through it, except for purely local access, and includes buffers against the adverse effects of general traffic. Few people want to live next to automobile parking areas and garages, even if attractively designed. Neither do they look upon automobile traffic near their homes as a desirable feature. Had the full extent of the adverse influences of the automobile on residential development been anticipated twenty years ago, a greater segregation of vehicular traffic movement and homes, except for purely individual access and servicing, would undoubtedly have been realized than is the case in many of our residential areas today. This very factor has been one of the important causes of residential blight.

The physical controls which can be used to regulate the automobile do not appear to be possible with the airplane, which cannot be confined within physical channels such as streets, freeways and parkways. It would appear that rigid regulations, strictly enforced, are the only alternative, and necessary regardless of the reduction of the noise factor. It is encouraging that the CAA is giving consideration to this problem.

8. City Services and Auxiliary Facilities.

(a) *Fire and Police Protection.* Careful consideration should be given to the present and potential availability of local fire fighting equipment and personnel. Adequate police protection should be assured either by the municipality or through community organization.

(b) *Schools.* A distance of one mile from home to elementary school is now considered too great, especially in the east with its higher population densities, and where major highway crossings are present or where the junior high school system is in use. School location within one-half mile radius and located off the major routes is becoming an accepted standard. If distances from home to school are substantially greater than ½ mile, school buses or good transit facilities should be available. Distances up to 2½ to 3 miles are satisfactory for high school. Public or private libraries within easy reach of both school and home are desirable adjuncts to any community development. Check these items with your local school authorities and planning commission as they relate to your project.

(c) *Recreation.* Trends in recreation areas are toward a separation of small children's playgrounds and larger recreation centers which include athletic fields, swimming pools, etc., for older age groups. The trend is also toward incorporating these facilities with the school building (which is used during off-school

25

periods) thus avoiding duplication of indoor facilities such as toilets, showers and gymnasium. Where separate school and recreation boards are established, arrangements for the cooperative use and supervision of the areas during and out of school hours have proved very successful, and the resulting economies in land, structures, and maintenance have been substantial. The Council recommends strongly that school and recreation facilities be contiguous and used cooperatively and that supervision be provided. Walking distances to recreation areas thus would correspond with those of the school. In any case, usable recreation areas should be within not more than fifteen minutes walking time without crossing major traffic arteries, unless adequate traffic lights or other safety features are provided at these points to protect the pedestrian. Small areas for pre-school children should be provided in addition to the above facilities and maintained by the local government or by a property owners' association.

(d) *Waste Disposal and Street Service.* Preference should be given to the site which is within an area of public or private refuse collection and, in the north, where municipal or other services supply snow removal and sanding of roadways.

(e) *Auxiliary Facilities.* Preference should be given to property conveniently served by already established semi-public and private institutions and facilities such as churches, hospitals, movies, and other commercial recreation, banks, laundry agencies, and other shopping service facilities. Those facilities used daily should be within walking distance of the development.

9. Municipal Regulations.

(a) *Zoning.* Comprehensive municipal zoning regulations are now in effect in about 80 per cent of the cities in the United States with a population in 1940 of 25,000 and over. Zoning has become a firmly established and accepted form of police power regulation with thirty years of experience and favorable legal opinion to establish its benefits and validity. Basically, zoning provides for the division of the municipality into a number of use districts within which the height, open space, building coverage, and more recently the density of population for respective districts are specified.

The Council is strongly in favor of zoning as a beneficial instrument in protecting residential neighborhoods against adverse uses and stabilizing community development and land values. However, many zoning ordinances and maps have been poorly drawn, are obsolete in many respects such as too many strip commercial districts, inadequate protection for residential neighborhoods and the like, and are often carelessly administered and amended through uninformed or politically minded city officials and councils. The aggregate result in many cities has been a piecemeal breaking down of comprehensive zoning through isolated ordinance and map changes and unrelated spot zoning with little or no reference to the overall plan for the city. The need for extensive modernization of obsolete codes and procedures in order to correct these and other deficiencies is becoming increasingly recognized and is strongly advocated by the Council. County zoning especially within metropolitan areas has received attention within recent years. Another desirable recent development is the provision in some ordinances for large scale community development which will permit a variety of housing types together with a local shopping center and certain other features if carried out as a unit in accordance with an overall community plan. While it is recognized that zoning does not create vested property rights, it is emphasized, however, that due consideration should be given by every zoning board to the economic factors involved in order to avoid confiscation of property values and create confidence in real estate investment and home ownership.

Zoning does not take the place of protective covenants and should not be confused therewith. One is a public police regulation, the other a private contract. Both are necessary to good community development. Private covenants are discussed in Part III.

Be sure to check zoning of land adjacent to any contemplated site as well as that of the site itself. Check the possibilities of obtaining zoning revisions if such changes appear desirable, such as inclusion of a local shopping center if justified by tributary population, elimination of string commercial zones and the like. The developer can often render effective service to his community as well as himself by calling attention to and working for the improvement of obsolete and poorly administered zoning ordinances and maps.

(b) *Subdivision Regulations.* Subdivision regulations, although more recent than zoning, have also become an accepted method of municipal and county control under the police power. In the introduction to his study, "Subdivision Regulations", Harold W. Lautner makes the following pertinent comment:

"The subdivider of a parcel of land does very much more than sell real estate by a bargain concerning the buyer and the seller alone. The results of his activities are in truth indelibly impressed upon the physical pattern of the community at large. What the subdivider of land does and how he does it are of extreme importance to the general public as well as to the individual. Rarely does a community lay out its own streets. Except in the case of main thoroughfares, most streets are located by the subdivider of land, the community sooner or later accepting these with the lots and blocks as laid out. The subdivider's primary motive in subdividing land is private profit, but the motive of the community, which sooner or later finds itself responsible for the subdivided land as a part of the whole machinery of the city, is public service. The necessity for coordination of these two desires is evident. The efforts, therefore, of our communities to regulate and guide the subdivision of land are a necessary part of their government and administration. The so-called subdivision regulations are manifestations of direct control of this activity by the community under the police power."

About 30 per cent of the cities in the United States of over 25,000 have authority to regulate subdivision development beyond their corporate limits ranging from one to ten miles, the most common being three miles. Before embarking on any development plan, the local regulations and procedures should be checked carefully, not only for subdivision design, but for improvement requirements which are commonly included. If land is involved upon which old but undeveloped subdivisions are recorded and streets dedicated, it may be possible in many cases to remove the recorded plat through complete ownership or through agreements with adjacent property owners affected.

As in zoning, subdivision regulations in many cities have become obsolete in the light of modern subdivision design. In addition, many regulation requirements are excessive with regard to such matters as street and roadway pavement widths, type and thickness of paving, and other items. The result has been to discourage development within the city in favor of the outlying areas, where in some cases regulations are more reasonable and modern than within the city, but in many cases are absent or wholly inadequate to assure a suitable residential community. There are, of course, instances in the outlying sections where requirements are so severe as to make the construction of modest homes impossible. Cities and counties should study this matter seriously with the view of bringing about more comparable standards between inlying and outlying areas, and to bring their standards into line with modern design and construction.

Subdivision regulations will usually set up certain procedures and minimum design and engineering standards which in most modern ordinances include the following:[1]

1. Submission of a preliminary and final plat of subdivision for approval prior to plat recording. This procedure includes regulations as to plat preparation, fees and costs, time schedules for submission, approvals and public hearings, and dedication of streets and open spaces.

2. Standards and Design Requirements. These regulations establish certain maximum and minimum criteria covering:

   a. Streets; their location, width, alignment grades, intersection, use of culs-de-sac, relation to the city street system and street trees, building lines, alleys, easements, etc.

   b. Blocks; length, width, cross walks, and utility easements.

   c. Lots; size, shape, and minimum dimensions.

   d. Open spaces; character, and area required for dedication, if any.

   e. Zoning and private covenants and their relation to subdivision regulations.

   f. Variations and exceptions.

   g. Subdivision names.

3. Requirements relating to drafting standards, form of presentation, and information required to be shown on preliminary and final plats.

4. Requirements on grading plans and profiles.

5. Improvements required in the development. These requirements usually include tract and street monuments, street grading, surfacing or paving, curbs, gutters and sidewalks, storm and sanitary sewers, culverts and bridges, water mains, and in infrequent cases, the location of utility lines and installation of gas mains. (See discussion on pages 76-81.)

---

[1] Detailed information on modern subdivision regulation practice will be found in "Subdivision Regulations" by Harold W. Lautner, published by Public Administration Service, Chicago, Illinois, upon which the above list is based.

(c) *Building Codes.* Building codes are mainly concerned with structural requirements and arrangement of buildings for health and safety, but they may enter into the consideration of sites and lotting relative to such items as attached garages, building height, required exits, and facilities in shopping centers. Be sure to check your building code against the zoning ordinance as its provisions sometimes govern where overlapping regulations occur.

As in zoning, many building codes are badly in need of revision to meet modern building trends. On this subject J. C. Nichols says: "Our builders and community developers should take an active interest in securing good building, sanitary, and subdivision regulations. The building codes of many of our cities are obsolete, drawn to favor certain industrial trades and certain types of merchandise, creating unnecessary cost in home construction. Certainly our city building codes should permit within the city limits such types of construction as are approved today by F.H.A." Such codes should not be too drastic or create excessive construction costs.

10. City Departments.

L. F. Eppich of Denver emphasizes the need to check with the local planning commission on planned future extensions of streets and other transportation facilities, parks and playgrounds, and questions pertaining to ordinance and code requirements. Check also with the building inspector, sewer and highway department and zoning board for their detailed requirements; the school board for extension or modification of school facilities; and the health department on stream pollution, mosquito control, sewage disposal and water supply.

11. Attitude of City Government.

The larger the development the more important it is that the mayor, council members and county officials be consulted and an attitude of good will obtained. This may be done directly, but preferably by working with or through the planning commission. It is strongly recommended that before purchase and development of modest homes, the local Federal Housing Administration officials be consulted even though no residential building is to be done by the operator. Their advice regarding site selection, planning, and protective covenants will be found to be of great value in helping to avoid costly errors later. F.H.A. approval is a great asset for low and medium priced projects.

12. Methods of Purchasing Land in Large Acreage.

(a) *General.* Where the developer does not acquire all of the land he intends to develop at the start of his project, a plan which sets forth the general scheme of the development should be approved by the owner of the acreage involved, and an agreement entered into setting forth the acreage prices to be paid for the entire property. An owner can usually be shown that it is good business to enter into an agreement with the developer which will insure to the developer the necessary protection and incentive to proceed with a long term program. David Bohannon of San Francisco discusses this aspect of land assemblage in the following statement:

"In most communities, there are holdings of undeveloped acreage which are feasible to develop, but due to the reluctance of the developer to purchase the entire property and the inability of the owner to develop his own property, nothing happens but an accumulation of taxes. Even where the owner of extensive acreage is willing to sell the amount of property which the developer feels he can immediately absorb, it results in poor planning and possible negative effect upon the value of the remaining acreage.

"A community builder and land developer must invest a substantial amount of capital in the preparation of a master plan, in order to insure a sound, well balanced community. To insure the highest use of the land and establish the initial program, he must frequently invest an amount of money entirely out of proportion to the number of acres first subdivided. There is usually an extensive advertising program, as well as physical installations required.

"An owner can be shown that it is good business to enter into an agreement with the developer that will give him the necessary protection and incentive to proceed with a program that may take a number of years to complete. The land owner can well afford to set an arbitrarily low price on a portion of the original acreage, in order to assist the developer in making ends meet through the costly pioneering period.

"First, a master plan that merely sets forth the general scheme of the development should be approved by the owner, and an agreement entered into setting forth the acreage prices of the entire property. The owner must recognize the fact that the initial investment on the part of the developer will increase his remaining acreage value, due to the kind of planning that is

31

undertaken. The owner must also realize that it is to the developer's interest to proceed as rapidly as the market will permit, and since he has little control over the market, he must be protected against a possible period of inactivity where he will have his initial effort and capital frozen for some time.

"It is obviously not to the land owner's interest to freeze the developer out because he cannot meet the requirements of an annual purchase. First, the number of years that it will take to develop the property under normal conditions should be estimated. On a large property, this should be at least ten years and preferably fifteen years.

"It is often argued that the developer should agree to purchase a given pre-determined number of acres which it would normally be expected he could absorb. It is proper that the owner have some protection against the freezing of his property when a developer fails to carry out his program. To meet this contingency, the owner should require a relatively small purchase each year in order to continue the option. Obviously, if the developer is inactive, he would not care to purchase additional acreage. Thus, the owner would be released from his agreement. On the other hand, if the developer is in good faith, but finds that market conditions are such that it is not feasible to carry out an active program within any given period, he can protect his investment by making the small purchase required. Thus, when conditions are again favorable, he can proceed with increased effort to place his inventoried property. Without this protection, the developer would hesitate to make the essential investment necessary to establish a project as a complete community development.

"The developer should also be privileged to purchase any amount of acreage he desires, to the end that he may freely carry out his engineering and land planning program. In the event the developer purchases an amount of acreage over and beyond a minimum requirement, he should be permitted to apply the excess purchase to future periods. It is important for the land owner to understand that it is to his interests to give the developer every reasonable protection, as it will encourage the developer in making a far more substantial investment in his initial operations than would otherwise be justified."

(b) *Options and Purchase Contracts*. Purchase contracts should be made to cover relatively long periods. Sliding scale options are very advantageous. In some cases it may be necessary to pay a nominal rent to keep the option alive. The danger of loading up with carrying charges on large tracts cannot be too strongly emphasized. Developers who sign purchase money paper for large acreage create a very dangerous liability. J. C. Nichols says on this subject: "Don't agree to short time payments on land you buy for development—15 to 20 years is desirable with reasonable release clauses. Many of us have made the mistake of agreeing to short time payments. If possible, carry future purchases on option basis with as small annual payments as possible. In purchasing your future land, try to get payments on principal and interest delayed if you expend certain agreed amounts on installing improvements on unreleased land."

(c) *Release Clauses.* The developer should be able to release any acreage of lots and streets that he needs. He should avoid tying himself up to releasing large blocks at a time.

Commenting on experiences in developing the Country Club District of Kansas City, J. C. Nichols says: "Do not fail to anticipate large increased taxes on land held for future development. This occurs because of greatly increased assessed valuations due to successful nearby developments. Tax assessors should not so penalize land held for future developments, but should assess it at wholesale land value.

"Do not assume that your assessor will not unduly tax your unsold lots in a subdivision. This unjustified increase of taxes has broken more good subdividers than any other factor. Unsold lots in the hands of a developer are still wholesale raw land and should not be assessed as lots until sold for a more intensive use.

"The State of Florida has proposed a very good law by which unsold land in a subdivision may be assessed only on an acreage basis until a reasonable percentage of all the lots are sold for residential purposes. This would be a wise law for all states to adopt. Don't forget that the last lots sold, if carried over a number of years with interest compounded, may not even repay your carrying charges to say nothing of the original cost of land and improvements."

PART II
Planning the Development

A. SITE INFORMATION FOR PLANNING.

1. Survey Maps.

There are four kinds of site data required before site planning and development can be intelligently started. These data cover property lines, topography, utilities and site location. The first three kinds of information are obtained by field surveys and can often be combined on one map.

(a) *Property Line Map.* This map should usually be at a scale of 1 inch equals 100 feet and should show the following information:

1. Bearings, distances, curve data, and angles of all outside boundaries and of block and individual parcel boundaries.

2. Location and dimensions of any connecting streets along the boundary of the property and the intersection lines of any adjoining tracts.

3. Any encroachments on outside boundaries as determined by survey.

4. All streets, alleys, or easements within or contiguous to the property with deed or dedication reference.

5. Names of record owners or reference to recorded subdivisions of adjoining property.

6. Any corner stones, pipes or other physical boundary markers as determined by survey.

7. All U. S., county, or other official bench marks, monuments or triangulation stations within or adjacent to the property, with precise position and description noted.

8. Computed area of all parcels comprising the property in square feet or acres.

9. True and magnetic meridian on the date of survey.

Permanent stone or concrete monuments should be set at each corner or angle on the outside boundary if not already so established. FHA requirements call for complete information on this point.

(b) *Topographic Map.* Where the site is rough, separate property and topographic maps may be desirable. Topographic maps should show the following data at a scale of not less than 1 inch equals 100 feet:

1. Contours—

   (a) One-foot interval where average slopes are 3 per cent or less.

   (b) Two-foot interval where slopes are up to 15 per cent.

   (c) Five-foot interval where slopes are over 15 per cent.

2. All existing buildings and other structures such as walls, fence lines, culverts, bridges, roadways, etc., with spot elevations where indicated.

3. Location and spot elevation of rock outcrops, high points, water courses, depressions, ponds and marsh areas, with any previous flood elevations as may be determined by survey.

4. Size, variety, caliper and accurate location of all specimen trees worth saving, and outline of all wooded areas.

5. Boundary lines of property.

6. Location of any test pits or borings if required to determine subsoil conditions.

Sufficient accuracy can usually be obtained and sometimes money saved by employing a stadia or plane table survey rather than a cross section survey in obtaining the above data.

(c) *Public Utilities Map.* It is sometimes desirable where the amount of data would make combined maps confusing to provide a separate map at a scale of 1 inch equals 100 feet showing by type:

1. All utility easements or rights-of-way.

2. Location, size and invert elevations of existing sanitary sewers, storm drains or open drainage channels, catchbasins and manholes.

3. Location and size of existing water, gas and steam mains, and underground conduits.

4. Location of existing overhead telephone and electric service and trunk lines, street and alley lighting with pole locations.

5. Location of streetcar or other rail lines.

6. Location of police and fire alarm boxes and similar appurtenances.

(d) *Site Location Map.* This map should be prepared at a smaller scale and with a view to possible later adaptation in advertising the development, and should include the following information:

1. Location of site with reference to the principal existing and proposed streets and principal approach or approaches.

2. Location and type of built-up areas in the vicinity.

3. Size and extent of nearby shopping centers.

4. Location and type of employment centers.

5. Location and type of transportation lines.

6. Location of churches, schools, parks, playgrounds and other educational and recreational facilities.

7. Zoning and covenants covering adjacent land and approaches to the site.

8. Jurisdictional boundaries.

9. Mile or half mile circles radiating from the site.

B. PLANNING THE SITE.

1. Site Planning.

Planning the subdivision, or site planning, involves the determination of the specific uses for definite areas of land and the planning of these areas in such a manner that the structures, the means of access and communication, the vehicular and pedestrian traffic, the open areas for recreation, and the areas for houses or other uses are coordinated to produce a unified development which can be built economically, operated efficiently, and maintained or marketed at normal expense. It is a technique which requires the assistance of a person or persons qualified by training and experience in this particular field. (See Part I, B.) It is upon a well ordered arrangement of land and ground forms that the engineering and architectural features are constructed.

2. Neighborhood Planning.

The creation of well balanced, self-contained communities should be the objective of all subdividers and operative builders. This can be accomplished more easily when a large tract is under one ownership, but the development of a complete neighborhood is not precluded even when there are several small subdivisions in separate ownership in the area. By careful, cooperative planning they can be integrated into a development which will eventually form a complete community of homes, schools, shops, recreation, and other facilities. "Let us so plan and build," advises J. C. Nichols, "in order to create stable values and neighborhoods of such permanent character as to endure for generations."

Figure 6.

An Example of Cooperative Effort Among a Group of Developers and Builders.

MIDWEST CITY, Oklahoma County, Oklahoma

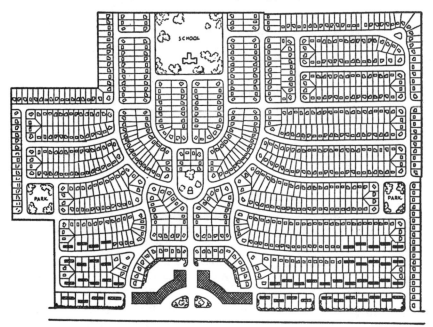

The developer of land for residential use must keep the neighborhood concept continually in mind from the standpoint of profit and of sound growth of his city. Isolated projects of small acreage and bearing little or no relation to the neighborhood idea are becoming a thing of the past. It is, of course, rare that a complete and properly integrated neighborhood can be created on less than 200 acres. As this is a greater acreage than the average developer can handle, it is recommended that land

38

in or contiguous to a neighborhood already started should be selected or that several operators pool their resources to create a complete neighborhood. This latter method has been used successfully at Midwest City, Oklahoma, where in 1942 sixteen builders and subdividers combined to create a community of a thousand homes. Each of the builders undertook the construction of separate portions of the project in accordance with the overall community plan. The sponsor, William P. Atkinson, assumed responsibility for streets, water system, business center, and similar facilities. (See Figure 6.)

The experience with Midwest City has been so successful that the same group of developers with some additions and changes are undertaking another project adjacent to Midwest City comprising more than 500 acres. This will be a real cooperative project with each of the developers assuming his proportionate responsibility and share in the entire project.

As noted by Newton Farr of Chicago, the neighborhood concept in planning new sections of cities or in replanning old areas is being developed on a city-wide basis by a number of planning commissions, notably in Chicago where the master plan of land use contemplates the progressive establishment of 59 community units each containing between 5 and 15 neighborhoods. Their size, type, boundaries and community facilities have been determined on the basis of existing physical barriers and an exhaustive land use survey, and modified in accordance with plans for future major thoroughfares, transportation, parks and playgrounds, and other planning considerations.

A complete and self-contained neighborhood unit of sufficient population should have its own local shopping center, elementary school and recreation facilities. It can be bounded by main traffic arteries but preferably not cut by them. Local streets within the neighborhood should be designed to serve the local needs of the neighborhood and to discourage their use by through traffic. Normally, two or more dwelling types (single family, two-family, apartments, etc.) and densities should be provided in appropriate locations. Figure 7 indicates generally accepted neighborhood unit principles. It is doubtful if a development has ever been planned which would secure the complete approval of all planners or developers. Compromises must always be made. Only wide experience, thorough knowledge of local markets, topography, and environing conditions can provide the basis for these compromises. No plans shown in this volume are presented as "perfect" plans. They illustrate certain phases of good planning.

39

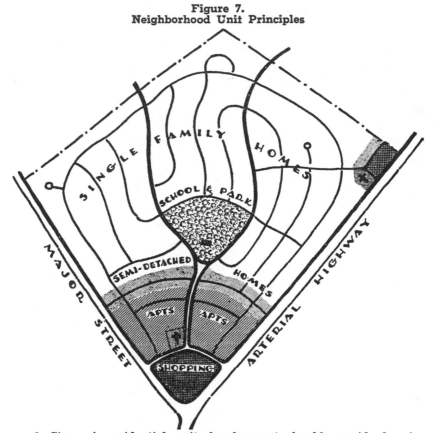

Figure 7.
Neighborhood Unit Principles

1. *Size.* A residential unit development should provide housing for that population for which one elementary school is ordinarily required, its actual area depending upon its population density.

2. *Boundaries.* The unit should be bounded on all sides by arterial streets, sufficiently wide to facilitate traffic by-passing the neighborhood instead of passing through it.

3. *Open Spaces.* Small park and recreation space, planned to meet the needs of the particular neighborhood, should be provided.

4. *Institution Sites.* Sites for the school and other institutions having service spheres coinciding with the limits of the unit should be suitably grouped about a central point, or common.

5. *Local Shops.* One or more shopping districts, adequate for the population to be served, should be located preferably at traffic junctions and adjacent to similar districts, if any, of adjoining neighborhoods.

6. *Internal Street System.* The unit should be provided with a special street system, each highway being proportioned to its probable traffic load, and the street net as a whole being designed to facilitate circulation within the unit with good access to main arteries, and to discourage its use by through traffic.

Adapted from New York Regional Plan, Vol. 7

3. Dwelling Density.

Table 5 shows densities for several types of dwellings with various lot sizes. The total acreage of the site less any unuseable or non-residential areas multiplied by the density figures shown in the table will give the approximate number of dwelling accommodations.

4. Price Range and Dwelling Types.

Maurice Read states that opinion on limiting the construction of homes to a narrow income group in any given project is rapidly changing. Better balanced residential communities and greater stability may often be obtained by having houses of various prices in a single community.

Table 5.

Dwelling Type	Lot Size Per Dwelling Unit In Feet	Net Density Dwellings/Acre*
	70 x 140 lots	3.1
	60 x 125 "	4.3
Detached houses	50 x 100 "	6.5
Semi-Detached houses, one-story	30 x 125 "	8.7
Semi-Detached houses, two-story	26 x 125 "	10.0
Row houses, one-story	20 x 100 "	16.3
Row houses, two-story	16 x 100 "	20.4
Garden Apartments, two-story		15 — 25
Garden Apartments, three-story		25 — 35
Apartments, multiple story		50 or more

"The more intensive the use of land, the greater need there is for wider streets, wider sidewalks, shorter blocks and particularly sufficient off-street parking space. The developer of such areas has a responsibility in making such sections of his city fitting, appropriate and serviceable to his community.

"Careful consideration should be given to not creating too great land coverage and too high population density. Intrusions into single residential areas should be avoided. Relationship of such intensive developments to shopping centers becomes extremely important. Nearby walk-in trade is a great support to such shopping centers. This more intensive population certainly needs nearby play and recreational areas." J. C. Nichols.

---

* Net density represents total number of dwellings per acre within the site, after deducting 25 per cent of site allocated to streets, park and recreation areas.

Similar opinion with regard to a reasonable diversity of housing types within the neighborhood is developing. A well balanced neighborhood plan containing a reasonable variation of housing accommodations will aid materially in stabilizing values and preventing decline by permitting the individual family to adjust its housing requirements to its age, marital status and size at any given time and still remain within the community of its choice.

Figure 8.
An Example of Good Community Design.

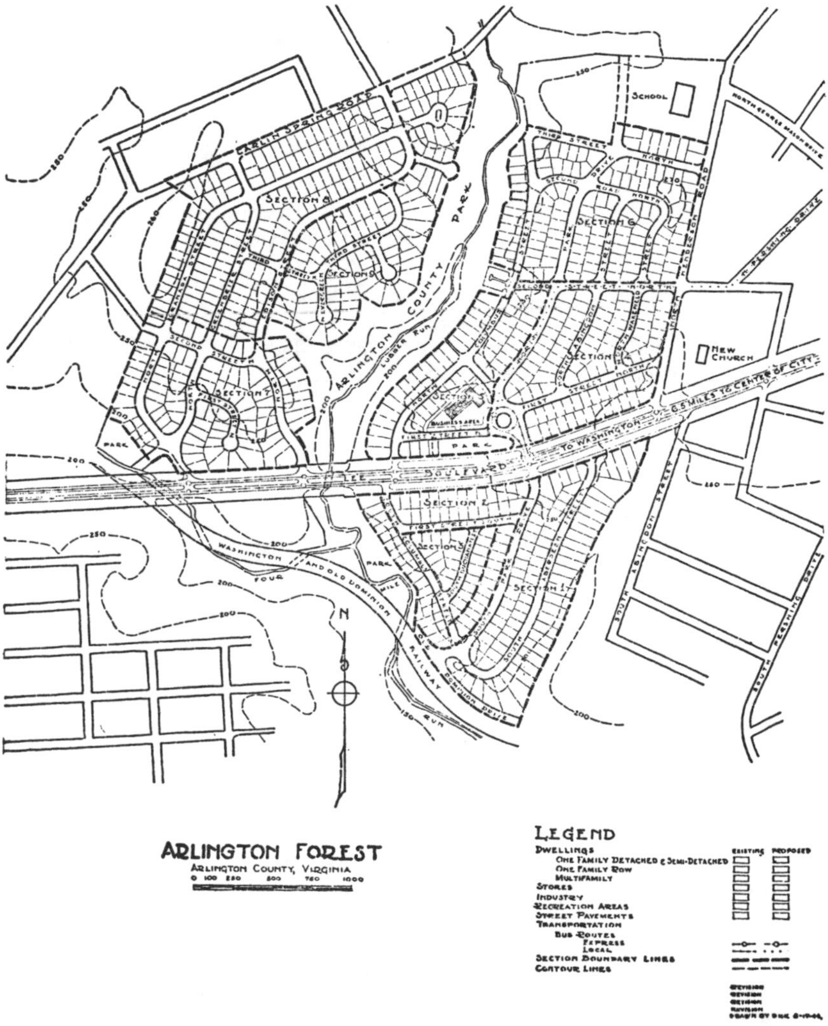

ARLINGTON FOREST
ARLINGTON COUNTY, VIRGINIA
0 100 250 500 750 1000

In developing the diversified community, it is recommended, however, that homes with too great a variance in price range or type not be mixed. In a small project of approximately 100 units or less a fairly narrow price range would undoubtedly be the wisest procedure. Where a complete neighborhood of several hundred units is being created, a variation in price range would be desirable. Based on 1940 construction costs, well designed homes costing 8 to 10 thousand dollars could be successfully blended with homes costing 15 thousand and over. Five to six thousand dollar homes blended with those costing 8 to 10 thousand is not considered too wide a variation. It is better to graduate by devoting both sides of a street or a section to each group with careful transition between. Good architectural design can, of course, make up for a considerable variance in construction costs.

In this connection John Mowbray says: "In a large development it is rarely wise to have houses all in one price range. Neighborhoods of low and medium, and medium and high priced homes can be attractively blended if carefully planned. The gradual transition need not be offensive if sufficient care is taken with the architectural design of the houses and careful attention given to site planning.

"Houses facing each other should be of the same general price, class and quality. The observer should not be conscious of a sharp transition or values will be adversely affected in the higher priced group."

5. Multi-Family Development.

(a) Multi-Family Units in the Community Development.

As noted in the discussion on neighborhood planning, recent trends in neighborhood units favor the inclusion of varied types of residential accommodations. The inclusion of apartment or multi-family units should normally be confined to developments of a thousand units or more which then become large enough to form complete communities.

A good location for multi-family units is adjoining a shopping center or grouped on thoroughfare frontage. It is not good planning to scatter them through a single-family area. It is usually desirable to place a buffer, such as a park, school, or church between apartments and single-family homes. The use of well designed double houses between the apartment and single-family areas often provides a good transition. It is usually best to permit the same type of land use on both sides of a street. The change of use will then be at the rear lot line instead of the street line.

The desirable ratio of multi-family to single-family dwellings will depend to a considerable extent on the location of the project, present and future market demand, and local custom. In general it is desirable to keep the ratio low. Overall metropolitan district averages indicate that the number of existing multi-family units of all types range from approximately 73 per cent in the New York area to 13 per cent in Fresno, California, of the total number of accommodations of all types in these areas. The actual area occupied by multi-family units is relatively small, however.

In outlying communities the so-called garden type apartment is recommended. Three stories is the maximum height which should be considered in this type of development, with the exception of occasional multiple story apartments where properly designed to conform with the surrounding development.

One of the desirable attractions of the garden apartment is the arrangement and amount of outdoor space provided. Where possible this space should be kept free from parking, and service features should be carefully grouped.

Ample off-street parking space should be provided in addition to curb parking. The amount necessary will vary with the type of building occupancy, and local conditions. Diagonal curb parking in connection with apartment development has been used satisfactorily in various parts of the country where located on local streets, and has been successful on heavily travelled streets in the Country Club District of Kansas City where a minimum 70 foot roadway was provided. It is suggested that you check your local regulations on this matter.

With outside living space on the rear and parking on the street side or in compounds, it is feasible to provide kitchen facilities on the street side with the living room having outside access on the open park space. In the vertical type apartment, flexibility in size of units can be obtained by arranging the second floor plan in such a way that one of the bedrooms is interchangeable with the adjacent unit. Trash and garbage receptacles in the kitchen wall adjacent to the front door permit easy collection service.

This type of multi-family development reduces project maintenance to a minimum by eliminating common halls and stairs,

44

**Plate II.
An excellent
garden-type
apartment.**

Entrance to
OLENTANGY
VILLAGE,
Columbus,
Ohio.

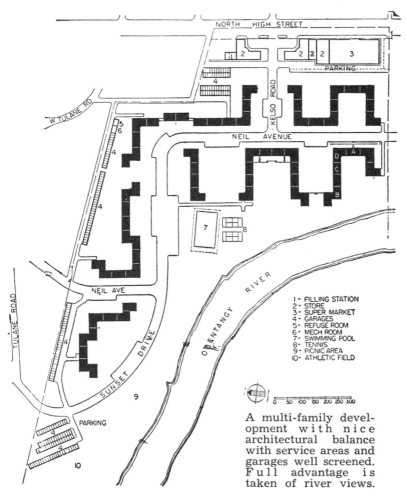

Figure 9.

Site Plan
for
OLENTANGY
VILLAGE

1 - FILLING STATION
2 - STORE
3 - SUPER MARKET
4 - GARAGES
5 - REFUSE ROOM
6 - MECH ROOM
7 - SWIMMING POOL
8 - TENNIS
9 - PICNIC AREA
10 - ATHLETIC FIELD

A multi-family devel-
opment with nice
architectural balance
with service areas and
garages well screened.
Full advantage is
taken of river views.

and trash collection, and affords living accommodations comparable to single family dwelling development.

6. Allocation of Land Use.

The amount of area to be allocated to streets, shopping center, recreation, etc., will depend on the number and density of families and type of dwelling as well as on the physical characteristics of the site. In general, areas allocated to non-residential uses within the neighborhood should not exceed 25 to 35 per cent of which approximately 20 per cent should be in streets and 3 to 5 per cent in the shopping center. Recreation areas should seldom be less than two to two and one-half acres in extent if they are to be of any great value to the community. Small children's play lots, however, can contain as little as 4 or 5 thousand square feet.

Schools and recreation areas for older children should be internal to the development except where they are designed to serve more than one neighborhood and should be combined as discussed on page 25. Rough land such as stream valleys not adaptable to building development, will often lend itself to park use. Steep hillside sites are not of much value for active recreation areas, however, and school and playground sites should be reasonably level or capable of being made so without undue grading. It is seldom advisable to locate either of these uses directly on a heavily traveled highway. Libraries usually desire an easily accessible location near a main thoroughfare, and form a good buffer between business and residential areas.

7. Block Size and Arrangement.

Local custom and regulations will often have as much influence on the size and shape of blocks as does the physical character of the site. Some cities still require that new streets shall be continuations of existing streets and that straight alignment be adhered to without proper regard for topography. This type of planning forces blocks into rigid patterns for the sake of uniformity and is highly undesirable for a residential neighborhood.

Plate III. Elevator Apartments Used as a Buffer Between the Shopping Plaza and Single Family Development. The parkway in the foreground also provides an excellent additional buffer between apartments and the commercial area.
COUNTRY CLUB DISTRICT, Kansas City, Mo. J. C. Nichols Co.

Fritz Burns of Los Angeles states that desirable block patterns permit blocks up to 1,800 feet long and under proper conditions, up to 2,000 feet. In general, long blocks should lie in the direction of the main local traffic flow and not cause long detours in reaching major objectives such as the school, bus stop or store group. Cross walks originally considered as desirable in long blocks have in actual practice proven impractical. They are disliked by abutting property owners, and unless actually needed because of peculiar circumstances, are little used and are difficult and expensive to maintain. Of the cross walk J. C. Nichols has this to say: "We dedicated and improved several pedestrian ways in long blocks. As a general rule they have not proved desirable. Adjoining home owners fear thieving and vandalism from narrow pedestrian ways near their homes. If such pedestrian ways are built, we suggest omission of all adjoining planting. Only in extreme cases do we feel they are justified." Similar experience of other members leads the Council to strongly recommend that, except in very unusual situations, cross walks be eliminated from residential development.

According to Van Holt Garrett of Denver, use of long blocks eliminates unnecessary cross streets, and in some cases, may produce up to a 20 per cent saving in street and utility costs over the short block plan, and provides more front selling feet. Based on years of satisfactory experience with the long block, members of the Council urge that municipal authorities revise their subdivision requirements, where necessary, to permit block lengths up to 2,000 feet with proper regard for storm drainage and local focal points already mentioned, thereby promoting economies in development and maintenance and greater freedom from intersectional traffic hazards.

The so-called super block plan, consisting of large deep blocks penetrated by a series of cul-de-sac service drives and with sidewalks located in a common interior park area, has not proved satisfactory in experimental projects in this country.

This planning pattern, as well as many of the "Greenbelt" schemes, is an adaptation of the English garden city layout and is a favorite proposal with student planners and others seeking to break with conventional patterns.

Such schemes call for communal action and close cooperation of the individual families over a long period. In the main they have been successful only where the dwelling units are leased with central maintenance or where there is strong control such as in a company town.

Careful analysis and comparison of all development costs show that the much heralded economies of the super block plan have not been borne out, and that there is a very definite resistance to such communal schemes on the part of the American home buyer. They are not recommended by the Council.

8. Lots.

(a) *Lot size.* Lot sizes for single house units vary considerably in various sections of the country. Local custom is an important factor, and minimum lot size and width may be set by local subdivision or zoning regulations. In Detroit and in many southern cities, lots of greater depth than 100 feet are desired, while 100 foot depth lots are the accepted standard in some west coast cities. Where the houses are all built by the developer, shallower lots may be used with careful house planning and design. Where lots only are to be sold, somewhat more ample dimensions are desirable to allow for purchasers' individual preferences.

In sections of California, low priced properties have been satisfactorily developed with lots no more than 90 feet in depth. In the north where two-story houses are customary, the minimum size lot recommended is 60 x 120 feet. In the south and west with their hot summers, or where one-story "ranch type" houses are customary, at least 65 to 70 foot lot widths are recommended. With regard to lot size, David Bohannon states: "If you are selling lots as such, they should be at least 60 x 125 feet, but if you are going to build the houses, you can use a shallower lot. There will be no sales resistance if the house is carefully planned and designed." Robert Jemison of Birmingham states that custom-built ranch-type houses are going to require much wider lots than have previously been offered.

According to John Mowbray, the normal length of a detached house lot should be about twice its width. Lots 60 x 120, 75 x 150, or 100 x 200 feet make good building sites. Steep topography frequently necessitates unusually deep lots, and very careful planning is necessary to use the land efficiently. Lots of too great depth, especially for modest priced homes, should be avoided as the excess depth is not used and becomes unsightly through lack of maintenance. Generally, wide shallow lots have better market appeal than narrow deep lots, but the cost of street improvements

Figure 10.

Existing streets and property lines are often controlling factors.
Several common mistakes made in lotting are shown below.

If the street can be relocated, it is worth the trouble.

When diagonal streets cannot be avoided:

Lot this way   Not this

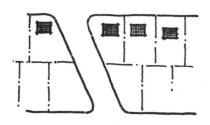 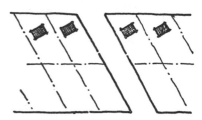

When existing intersecting streets form acute-angled intersections:

Lot this way   Not this

 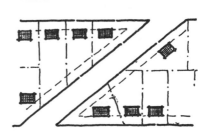

Where future street extensions are not required in corners of the property:

Lot in this manner   Not this

 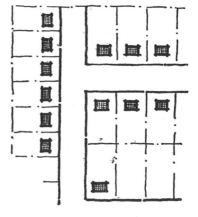

will be greater on the wider lots because of the increased frontage. Where row houses are common, shallower lots are acceptable with lot width of from 16 to 20 feet. However 90 to 100 feet should be considered a minimum depth. In general the minimum size of a lot should be based upon securing ample light, air, and driveway space, and upon fully meeting local customs and preferences.

"The cost to the developer of street and utility improvements is an important factor in controlling lot widths for low and medium priced developments," emphasizes Robert Gerholz of Flint, Michigan. In developments beyond the reach of city services where septic tanks and individual wells are used, minimum lot areas must be greatly increased in order to avoid possibility of contamination, nuisance and health hazards. Minimum requirements for sewage disposal systems will vary widely throughout the country depending on the composition of the subsoil and underlying rock. Minimum standards in such cases are usually prescribed by the local or state health authority.

(b) *Lot Lines.* The laying out of lots should not be done casually or left wholly to your engineer. Careful restudy of lot lines with due regard for topography can frequently result in thousands of dollars increased value by the creation of more desirable and usable home sites. This is more often possible where lots are larger with more flexibility in lot line location, but should by no means be overlooked in close development. Qualities which should be sought in lot layout as determined by lot line location should include:

1. A favorable site for placing the house. The question should always be asked—"Does the lot contain a good house site?"

2. Usable land to front and rear for lawn, garden, etc.

3. Adequate surface drainage away from house location with slopes generally toward the street or rear, with reasonable grade for garage and driveway approaches from the street.

4. Minimum amount of grading and retention of trees beyond the house location.

Side lot lines should be approximately at right angles to the street or radial to a curved street and, except where dictated by topography on large size lots, should be straight. Rear lot lines also should normally be straight and avoid acute angles with side lines except under special topographic conditions. On this point Wilburn K. Kerr of Columbus, Ohio, says that odd-shaped lots are hard to sell. Just a few such difficult lots and hangovers through the years can make your project a final loss. Streets that intersect at acute angles make poor shaped lots. They should be avoided. It is desirable that utility easements along rear lot lines be as straight and long as possible in order to avoid unnecessary manholes, poles, and guy wires at angle points.

(c) *"Butt" Lots.* Charles Joern of Chicago feels that butt lots are not desirable or economical except where the ends of blocks face lot frontages across a street. (See Figure 11.) Under the latter condition, the "butt" lot has the advantage of utilizing

Figure 11.

Diagram Showing Good and Poor Lotting Practice.

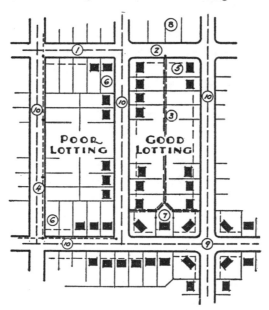

EXPLANATION

1. Excess underground utilities at end of block required.
2. No underground utilities at end of block.
3. Rear overhead utility easement.
4. Street overhead utilities.
5. Increased corner lot width.
6. Corner lots too narrow.
7. Good use of butt lot.
8. Butt lots require extra utilities with bad view down rear lot line.
9. Good lotting at street intersection.
10. Required underground utilities.

52

street utilities and closing the unsightly view down the rear lot lines in the block opposite.

Corner lots should be from 10 to 20 per cent wider than interior lots in order to provide an adequate yard space on the side street. A 10 to 15 foot differential in building setback between the side yard of the corner house and the front yard of the adjacent house on the same street is permissible depending on lot size. Where 25-foot front yards are required, at least a 15 foot side yard on the street side of the corner lot is desirable. Corner lots approximately square in shape permit diagonal placement of the house and provide both for a transition with the side street and an interesting grouping around the street intersection.

On this point Harry Taylor says: "Don't try to force buyers to acquire wider residential lots than they can afford to carry. We are all interested in creating the greatest possible free space around our homes, but must not be led into extravagant plans beyond the buyer's ability to pay and maintain."

J. C. Nichols observes: "Don't make the mistake of selling lots as narrow as 45 feet. We are now platting nothing less than 50 feet and are trying to hold a 60 foot minimum width for even the smallest house."

(d) *Lots Abutting Traffic Arteries.* When the property faces a heavy traffic street, there are several ways to protect residences from traffic noise and distraction. Most of these suggestions will increase improvement costs but create more desirable lots. From the traffic point of view it is highly desirable to keep both the number of individual driveways and the number of street intersections with main thoroughfares to a minimum.

1. Lay out deep lots with houses backing on the traffic way and screened from it by fence or wall and planting.[1]

2. Face houses toward the highway and lay out a planting strip 20 feet or more in width between the traffic way and an access street to serve the houses.

3. Construct short cul-de-sac or loop street, extending in from the highway with lots laid out so that no houses face directly on the traffic way.

---

[1] To be successfully done, the developer should erect the wall or fence and do the planting as part of the site development. This will insure a consistent treatment along the traffic frontage which is essential for appearance and permanency.

4. Face houses on the highway but with some additional setback, and service them from alleys or rear drives, permitting no individual driveway entrances to the highway.[1]

5. Face houses on the intersecting streets with driveways on the side streets, with kitchen and service on the highway side

Figure 12.

Methods of Subdividing Along Heavy Traffic Ways.

1. Backing on Traffic Way   2. Facing Traffic Way
                                                with Access Street

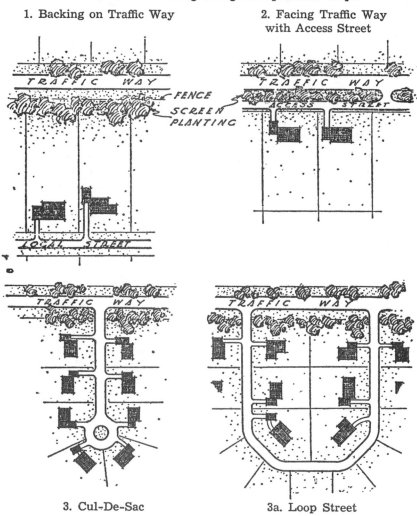

3. Cul-De-Sac   3a. Loop Street

---

[1] While some developers dislike this type of treatment, it has been successfully handled in a number of developments.

54

but opening on the rear yard. This, of course, will increase the number of street intersections on the main highway, but is usually less costly.

Local conditions and preferences will govern the method which will best serve the particular case. (See Figure 12.)

9. Building Lines.

Building lines may be set by subdivision regulations or by the zoning ordinance. The required dimensions should usually be considered as a minimum and not a standard. In any case, minimum building lines should be included in the protective covenants to assure adequate front yards and building setbacks, and to provide for better relationships among property owners, and between property owners and the community. The size and depth of the lot and character of the street will affect the amount of setback required. Building setbacks also depend upon street width, and may vary from five feet where hillside property is involved to as much as 50 feet or more on major highways to avoid noise, fumes and dirt. Setbacks of 25 to 30 feet on minor residential streets have become fairly standard. However, where the developer is constructing the houses, lesser setbacks of 20 or even 15 feet, in some cases, may be used satisfactorily if attention is given to proper house grouping and street width. Where living quarters are in the rear, lesser setbacks may be entirely satisfactory, particularly where one story structures are involved. Use of the integral curb and sidewalk will also increase the apparent setback of the house from the street; and the lesser setback creates more rear garden space. Economies are also obtained by shortened utility connections and drives to attached garages.

For greater interest, varied setbacks have been used placing building lines on alternate groups of lots back 5 to 15 feet. Care should be taken in the arrangement of setbacks. Do not stagger every other lot, but rather try to group the houses giving consideration to their architecture, the location of drives and service yards, and the alignment of the street. Varied setbacks are not necessary on curved streets, but will help to avoid a monotonous line when used on long straight streets.

Maurice Read suggests that it is an excellent idea to have your land planner and architect make a plan showing the location of each house on a street, possibly with a colored sketch of each house elevation, so that the relationship of the houses to each other is clearly evident. In a large housing project where

Figure 13.

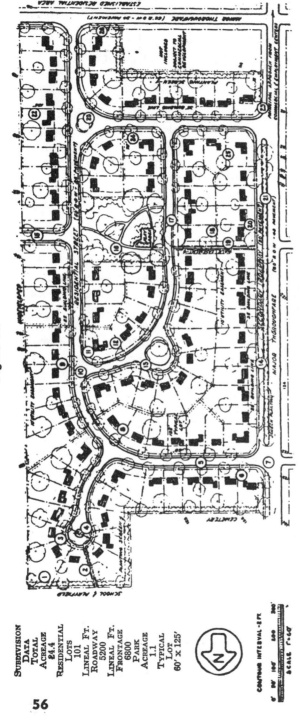

SUBDIVISION
DATA
TOTAL
ACREAGE 24.4
RESIDENTIAL
LOTS 101
LINEAL FT.
ROADWAY 5200
LINEAL FT.
FRONTAGE 6800
PARK
ACREAGE 1.1
TYPICAL
LOT 60' x 125'

CONTOUR INTERVAL - 2 FT.
0'   50' 100'   200'   300'
SCALE IN FEET

N

1. 15 foot easement for planting screen to provide protection from non-residential use.
2. 10 foot walk easement gives access to school.
3. Cul-de-sac utilizes odd parcel of land to advantage.
4. Turn-around right-of-way 100 feet in diameter.
5. Street trees planted approximately 50' apart where no trees exist.
6. Additional building set-back improves subdivision entrance.
7. Street intersections at right angles reduce hazards.
8. Lot side-line centered on street end to avoid car lights shining into residences.
9. Residences opposite street end set back farther to reduce glare from car lights.
10. Three-way intersections reduce hazards.
11. Property lines on 30' radii at corners.
12. Lot side-lines perpendicular to street right-of-way lines.
13. "Eyebrow" provides frontage for additional lots in deeper portion of block.
14. Secondary roadway eliminates hazard of entering major thoroughfare from individual driveways.
15. Provision for access to land now undeveloped.
16. Neighborhood park located near center of tract. Adjacent lots wider to allow for 15 foot protective side line set back.
17. Pavement shifted within right-of-way to preserve existing trees.
18. Above ground utilities in rear line easements.
19. 10 foot walk easement provides access to park. Adjacent lots wider to allow for 15 foot protective side line set back.
20. Variation of building line along straight street creates interest.
21. Screen planting gives protection from noise and lights on thoroughfare.
22. Lots backing to uncontrolled land given greater depth for additional protection.
23. Low planting at street intersections permits clear vision.
24. Wider corner lot permits equal building set back on each street.
25. Platting of block end to avoid siding properties to residences across street.
26. Lots sided to boundary street where land use across street is non-conforming.

Notes to Figure 13.

Subdivision Planning Standards.

The diagram opposite, prepared by the FHA, illustrates many of the standards advocated by the Community Builders' Council. Modifications of Items 2, 11 and 19 are indicated by experience. Plan indicates kind of information which should appear on any good development plan.

This subdivision provides 101 desirable building sites for low cost homes. A majority of the houses face east or west and will, therefore, receive sunlight into their front rooms at some time during the day. In the preparation of the plat for recording, lots should be numbered consecutively throughout the entire tract.

The street plan is adapted to the topography and provides for surface water drainage. Although the number of entrances from the major thoroughfare is limited, the street pattern facilitates the flow of traffic from the principal approach. Curved streets create greater appeal than is possible in a gridiron plan. Long blocks are desirable and reduce expense for cross streets. This subdivision does not require its own system of major thoroughfares. However, recognition is made of the present and planned roadway pattern of the city in which it is located.

A subdivision of this size does not require provision for complete community facilities, such as stores, schools, and churches, necessary in a larger neighborhood.

Complete information regarding the site and its relation to the town or city of which it is a part is essential to the planning of a desirable residential neighborhood. Not only is it necessary to have a closed, true-boundary survey, but also complete topographical data, including locations of existing trees that might be preserved. The capacity of storm and sanitary sewers should be known. The adequacy of a safe water supply system and the existence of other essential utilities, and of transportation facilities, are important factors.

Residential subdivisions should be located where they will not be adversely affected by industrial expansion and other non-conforming uses. They should be in the trend of residential development of similar type homes. To further assure stability, residential areas should be safeguarded by recorded protective covenants, and the establishment and enforcement of a zoning ordinance governing the use of the property and surrounding areas.

a limited number of house plans and elevations are used, this procedure will be found invaluable in selecting the house types which go well together.

Regarding corner lot setbacks, Hugh Potter of Houston states: "There should be a flexible arrangement for side yard setbacks on corner lots. We have been using 15 to 20 feet with the right of the developing company to reduce it if they so desire."

10. Streets.

"Major streets should conform to the master street plan for the community," advises L. F. Eppich. This may mean that a few of the more important streets of the community may have to be continued through the development and be of greater width. Other streets preferably should be planned to reduce their use for through traffic. Fire protection should be considered carefully and plans should be checked with local fire officials for hydrant location, cul-de-sac turn-abouts, access to buildings, etc.

The street pattern should relate properly to the major and secondary street plan and to site terrain. Natural drainage courses can often be used to advantage as street locations. Avoid a gridiron pattern of streets; it is monotonous, inefficient and generally costs more money.

(a) *Street Widths.* There is the tendency in many municipalities to require excessive widths for minor single family residential streets. This is reflected in a similar tendency to require excessive roadway pavements. The Council is of the opinion that minor street rights-of-way in detached residential neighborhoods should not exceed 50 feet with roadways not greater than 26 feet from face of curb to face of curb. This provides for two lanes of parallel curb parking and one lane for moving traffic which is entirely adequate for local circulation. The primary function of the minor residential street is that of access to abutting property and not for traffic movement as such. Provision of two moving lanes requires 33 to 34 feet of pavement, invites fast traveling, increases initial paving costs by about 20 per cent, and adds a like amount to future maintenance. A width of 26 feet also provides adequate space for cars in backing out of individual driveways which have proper radii.

On major residential streets which must act as collector streets for traffic originating in the neighborhood, on streets adjacent to shopping centers and other focal points, and where

Figure 14.

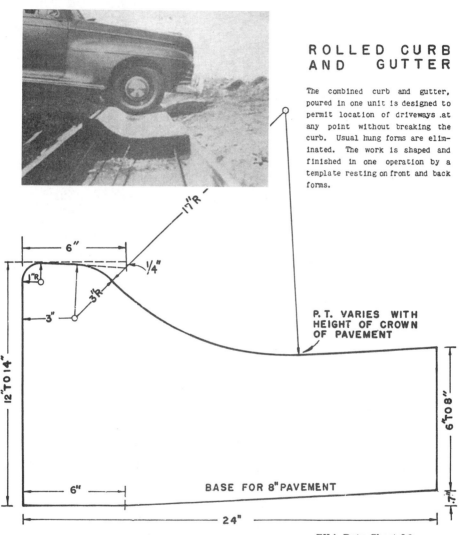

ROLLED CURB
AND GUTTER

The combined curb and gutter, poured in one unit is designed to permit location of driveways .at any point without breaking the curb. Usual hung forms are eliminated. The work is shaped and finished in one operation by a template resting on front and back forms.

17"R

6"

1/4"

1"R

3½R

3"

P. T. VARIES WITH
HEIGHT OF CROWN
OF PAVEMENT

12"TO 14"

6"TO 8"

6"

BASE FOR 8"PAVEMENT

.7"

24"

FHA Data Sheet L3

serving apartment developments, Judson Bradway of Detroit recommends 60-foot street widths with 33 to 34 foot pavement widths as satisfactory.

(b) *Sidewalks.* Many cities require the construction of sidewalks on both sides of the roadway in all residential subdivisions. However, on minor streets in single family areas, two sidewalks are frequently unnecessary and in open development of large lots of 100 foot frontage or more, sidewalks may be eliminated without objection. Fritz Burns, Los Angeles, questions whether sidewalks contribute to the safety of children as accidents usually occur when they run into the roadway or emerge from behind parked cars. Sidewalks tend to encourage use of the street for play rather than off-street areas such as the rear yard or playground. In general, the Council recommends a sidewalk on at least one side of the street.

On major residential streets which serve as collectors of traffic from minor streets, as approaches to the school, bus stop, shopping center, and other focal point of the community, and where densities exceed five families per net acre, sidewalks are usually needed on both sides of the street.

Four foot sidewalks are sufficient on minor streets, although sidewalks three feet six inches in width have proved entirely satisfactory where combined with rolled curbs. Greater widths are unnecessary except where leading and adjacent to shopping centers and other focal points. In any case all utilities such as poles and fire hydrants should be kept out of the paved area.

The integral sidewalk and curb is favored although its use in northern climates may complicate snow disposal, and this construction has been objected to for this reason by city engineers. Driveway aprons which break the sidewalk level are an objectionable feature of the combined sidewalk and vertical curb, but can be obviated by the use of the rolled curb. One feature to watch in the construction of the sidewalk contiguous to the curb is settlement. This may be avoided if the sidewalk subgrade is thoroughly prepared prior to placing.

(c) *Rolled Curbs.* Rolled curbs (see Figure 14) are favored by the majority of the Council and have been universally accepted in many parts of the country. They provide a pleasing

Plate IV. Good Use of Rolled Curb.
"HILLSDALE", San Mateo, California.

Table 6. Critical Clearance Dimensions of Selected Passenger Automobiles.

	A	B	C	D	E	F	G	H	I	J	K
			OVERHANG			GROUND CLEARANCE					
NAME	Overall Length (Feet)	Wheel Base (Feet)	Ctr. Rear Wheel to Rear Bumper (Feet)	Ctr. Front Wheel to Front Bumper (Feet)	Size of Wheel & Tire (Inches)	Ground to Exhaust (Inches)	Ground to Lowest Points (Inches)	Ground to Front Bumper (Inches)	Ground to Rear Bumper (Inches)	Turning Circle Average (Feet)	Overall Width (Feet)
1946 Chrysler—											
Crown Imperial—8 cyl.	19.6	12.1	3.8	3.6	7.50 x 15	9.5	7.0	12.8	13.2	48.2	6.3
Royal—6 cyl.	17.4	10.1	3.8	3.5	6.50 x 15	9.0	6.5	12.7	13.0	40.7	6.3
Desoto	17.3	10.1	4.0	3.2	6.50 x 15	9.0	6.5	12.5	13.5	40.5	6.3
Desoto 7 passenger	18.8	11.6	4.0	3.2	7.00 x 15	9.0	6.8	12.5	13.5	45.0	6.3
Dodge	17.1	10.0	4.0	3.1	6.00 x 15	9.0	6.5	13.3	13.3	40.2	6.8
Dodge 7 passenger	18.6	11.5	4.0	3.1	7.00 x 15	9.3	6.8	13.3	13.3	45.0	6.3
Plymouth	16.4	9.8	3.8	2.8	6.00 x 16	9.0	6.5	13.0	13.0	39.3	6.1
1946 Buick—"40"	17.3	10.1	4.2	3.0	6.50 x 16	6.1	6.0	16.4	15.9	42.7	6.5
Buick—"70"	18.1	10.8	4.3	3.0	7.00 x 15	.....	6.1	16.7	16.1	45.6	6.6
Cadillac 61	17.8	10.5	4.4	2.9	7.00 x 15	.....	6.6	16.1	14.4	45.7	6.7
Cadillac 75	18.9	11.3	4.7	2.9	7.50 x 16	.....	5.8	15.8	15.5	48.8	6.9
Chevrolet—St. Master	16.6	9.7	4.1	2.8	6.00 x 16	.....	7.3	16.3	15.8	42.3	6.1
Oldsmobile—66	17.0	9.9	4.1	3.0	6.00 x 16	.....	7.2	16.0	14.7	41.9	6.3
Oldsmobile—98	18.0	10.5	4.5	3.0	7.00 x 15	.....	7.1	16.0	15.9	46.0	6.5
Pontiac—25	17.0	9.9	4.2	3.0	6.00 x 16	.....	7.7	15.2	15.0	42.6	6.3
Pontiac—28	17.5	10.2	4.3	3.0	6.50 x 16	.....	6.3	14.6	16.2	41.7	6.4
1946 Lincoln	18.2	10.4	4.5	3.2	7.00 x 15	9.4	6.8	9.5	8.4	44.5	6.5
Mercury	16.9	9.8	4.0	3.0	6.50 x 16	8.8	7.5	11.2	12.1	41.0	6.1
*Ford	16.5	9.5	4.2	3.0	6.00 x 16	10.3	7.5	12.3	13.5	41.0	6.1
1947 Studebaker—											
14A—Commander	17.0	9.9	3.8	3.3	6.50 x 15	10.9	6.1	11.1	12.0	42.0	5.8
6G—Champion	16.0	9.3	3.8	2.9	5.50 x 15	10.0	5.9	12.7	10.4	42.9	5.8
1946 Nash—											
*"Ambassador 6"	17.4	10.1	4.0	2.8	5.00 x 15	8.0	8.0 Exhaust Pipe 9.0 Muffler	14.8	18.0	38.0	6.3
*Nash "600"	16.6	9.3	4.0	2.8	4.00 x 16	10.5	6.7	14.5	17.0	41.0	6.3
1946 Packard—2100-1-11	17.4	10.0	4.2	3.2	6.50 x 15	9.0	.....	11.0	10.8	42.0	6.3
2126	19.7	12.3	4.2	3.2	7.50 x 16	.....	.....	11.0	10.8	52.0	6.3
1947—Kaiser and Frazer	16.9	10.3	8.8	2.8	6.50 x 15	12.8	7.1	12.5	13.8	44.0	6.1

From data furnished by the Chrysler, General Motors, Ford, Nash, Studebaker, Packard, and Kaiser-Frazer Corporations.

* See notes on page 63.

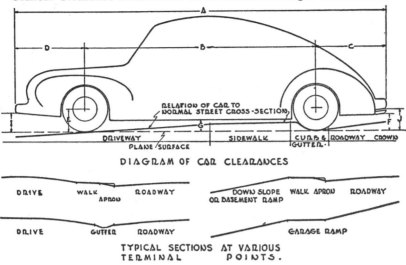

Diagram to Table 6.
Critical Clearance Dimensions of Selected Passenger Automobiles.

DIAGRAM OF CAR CLEARANCES

TYPICAL SECTIONS AT VARIOUS
TERMINAL POINTS.

NOTES TO TABLE 6: Dimensions have been converted into feet and nearest tenth to be directly comparable and easily used. Letters at head of each column refer to corresponding dimensions in the diagram.

Asterisk notes disparity between overall length and sum of B, C and D.

unbroken street line, do not require expensive curb cuts for driveways necessary with the straight curb, and are one of the most practical cost reducing items in street construction. The objection has been made that the rolled curb encourages automobile parking on the sidewalk or grass strip. This has not been found valid by Council members who have used it.

The rolled curb can be easily and quickly laid by use of a steel template with only front and back forms. At street intersections, curb returns with a radius of 15 feet are recommended. At such points, the rolled curb should be warped into a straight curb. This discourages corner cutting by automobiles and avoids the danger of slipping on a sloping surface at the pedestrian crosswalk, especially by women wearing high heels.

(d) *Car Clearances.* Concern has been expressed by the Council over the recent tendency among automobile designers to reduce the ground clearance and increase the overhang of recent models with the result that some current makes cannot clear ordinary changes in grade such as driveway aprons, rolled curbs,

Figure 15.

An Example. – Use of Culs-de-Sac and Loop Streets. Streets are laid out to conform to rough topography.

SUGGESTED SUBDIVISION PLAN FOR
WOODSIDE ACRES
REDWOOD CITY, SAN MATEO COUNTY CALIFORNIA
NOVEMBER 9, 1944

SCALE IN FEET

NOTE: See Fig. 26, Page 148, for Shopping Center Detail.

Source F. H. A.

commercial garage ramps, and streets in hilly areas, without damage to the car. It is recommended that developers investigate new car clearances when laying out new areas and advise residents in their developments of car models in which this difficulty is to be encountered. Table 6 shows the critical clearances of a number of current models, several of which have given trouble.

(e) *Culs-de-sac and Loop Streets.* Culs-de-sac or dead-end streets with turning space at the end are satisfactory when they are not over 500 feet in length and have a minimum turn-around of not less than 40 foot radii from center of circle to outside curb with a small grass space in the center. There is objection however to repeated use of them as they present problems of sewerage and drainage, dead-end water mains, and refuse collection. In multi-family or even intensive single family developments, where a considerable volume of traffic is generated, use of culs-de-sac is questionable as they require all entering traffic to turn and leave by the point of entry thereby approximately doubling the local traffic volume. The use of the Y or T "backaround" can sometimes be used to advantage on short culs-de-sac where a small number of lots are served. Excessive cuts to provide for the circle can thus be avoided and the central grass panel eliminated.

In many cases loop streets can be used to good advantage as they do not have the objectionable features of the cul-de-sac, but do contribute to privacy and discourage through traffic. Loop streets and culs-de-sac can also be used to advantage to pick up groups of lots in odd corners of the property, in the center of excessively deep blocks, or where topography or natural features make a normal street pattern difficult. A skilled land planner will not limit himself to a fixed pattern or stereotyped repetition of street and block treatment. Each development is a separate problem requiring not only adjusting the plan to the topography, but of recognizing local customs and market preferences. Further discussion on the excessive use of the cul-de-sac will be found on page 48.

(f) *Intersections.* Fairly sharp curb radii of approximately 15 feet at intersections on minor streets are desirable rather than longer radii which permit high automobile speeds in turning corners thereby endangering pedestrians. The amount of street paving is also reduced with resultant savings in paving costs.

Acute angle street intersections should be avoided where at all possible. They create excessive roadway paving, are traffic hazards, and create block shapes which are difficult and uneconomical to lot.

(g) *Driveways.* Driveways too commonly have little or no radius at their intersection with the curb or street pavement. However, proposals made by some traffic engineers to use curb radii for driveways up to twelve feet are entirely unsound. Such returns would not only be costly, but would require wide park strips between curb and sidewalk, occupy from 1/2 to 2/3 of the roadway frontage of the ordinary 50 to 60-foot lot, and invite excessive speeds in approaching or leaving individual driveways. Eight feet is considered the minimum driveway width with a 3 to 5-foot transition radius at the curb. Use of the rolled curb makes the provision of curb returns unnecessary.

Strip or ribbon driveways with a central grass panel have not proved satisfactory as they become unsightly, are difficult to maintain, and decrease construction costs very little if any.

(h) *Planting Strips Next to Curb.* Planting strips, where curbs and walks are separated, should be at least eight feet wide if street trees are to be planted. Five-foot strips are too narrow for proper tree growth. Tree roots eventually tend to heave sidewalks where narrow strips are used. The Council recommends planting street trees back of the sidewalk where root growth will not be restricted, unless adequate planting strips are provided.

11. Street Improvement Costs.

The cost of local improvements per lot will vary in different sections of the country and will also depend upon local requirements. Table 7 shows a breakdown of costs in five sections of the country as found in the Summer of 1947. As these are averages there will be considerable variation between the cities in each section. Costs have changed so rapidly since the war that these figures should be considered as a guide only and should be checked with local contractors.

Figure 16 shows a method of computing the total cost of an improved lot after raw land cost and street improvement costs are known. It should be noted that front foot costs should

Plate V. Note wide sloping gutters and absence of sidewalks.
CRESTMORE PARK, Denver, Colorado. Garrett-Bromfield & Co.

be expressed in terms of "selling" feet, i.e., to include in the cost per front foot of land to be sold, the costs of side street construction, plus the cost of any improvements abutting frontage to be dedicated for park, playground, or other open space use.

Another aspect of street costs is to be found in the comment of J. C. Nichols: "We were entirely too liberal in dedicating to our city wide parkways and boulevards through our properties in view of the fact that we were later assessed high special taxes for carrying these parkways and boulevards on through adjoining properties whose owners were not willing to dedicate their lands. The developer should be protected by some agreement with the city before making similar dedications."

12. Community Facilities.

(a) Future school and church sites should receive careful attention when establishing the general plan. The school location should be selected after consultation with the School Board, and from the developer's standpoint elementary schools should be as accessible as possible from all sections of his project. However, a location on a main traffic artery is generally not recommended. It is also poor policy to place the school in the choicest section as the noise and student activity are somewhat adverse factors unless well insulated from adjacent residential development.

School sites with ample playgrounds of at least 5 acres for elementary and 10 acres or more for high school are desirable. Sidewalks should be constructed on both sides of all streets leading to schools.

(b) Churches have proved undesirable when located among residences largely because of the automobile parking problem. Activities are going on continually in the modern church. Church sites adjacent to shopping centers have been found satisfactory where they act as a buffer between residential and business uses and where parking is provided nearby which will reduce the damaging effect of excessive parking on residential streets. However, churches should not be so located as to monopolize parking areas in shopping centers at times when shops are open for

Plate VI. **Attractive Treatment of Cul-de-Sac with Contiguous Curb and Sidewalk.**
"HOMELAND," Baltimore, Maryland, Roland Park Company.
John McC. Mowbray, President.

Table 7.

Average Front Foot Cost for Street Improvements in Subdivisions in 1947.

	Northeastern States[6]		Southeastern States[7]		North Central States[8]		Southwestern States[9]		West Coast States[10]	
	Unit Cost	Front Foot Cost[3]	Unit Cost	Front Foot Cost	Unit Cost	Front Foot Cost	Unit Cost	Front Foot Cost	Unit Cost	Front Foot Cost
Grading—Average 12" Cut	$1.00 cu. yd.	$ .50	$ .70 cu. yd.	$ .35	$ .90 cu. yd.	$ .45	.60 cu. yd.[12]	$ .30	$ .75 cu. yd.	$ .38
Paving—Base[11]	.80 sq. yd.	1.05	.75 sq. yd.	.96	1.60 sq. yd.[4]	2.05	.65 sq. yd.	.83	.70 sq. yd.	.90
Wearing Surface[11]	.55 sq. yd.	.71	.50 sq. yd.	.64	.50 sq. yd.	.64	.50 sq. yd.	.64	.90 sq. yd.	1.15
Curb and Gutter—Cement Concrete, Rolled or Straight Faced	1.50 lin. ft.	1.50	1.40 lin. ft.	1.40	1.65 lin. ft.	1.65	1.30 li. ft.[12]	1.30	1.50 lin. ft.	1.50
Sidewalks—Cement Concrete 4" x 4"	.30 sq. ft.	1.20	.30 sq. ft.	1.20	.35 sq. ft.	1.40	.30 sq. ft.[12]	1.20	.30 sq. ft.	1.20
Sanitary Sewer—Minimum 8"	2.75 lin. ft.	1.38	2.50 lin. ft.	1.25	2.10 lin. ft.	1.05	2.30 lin. ft.	1.15	2.25 lin. ft.	1.13
Storm Drainage[1]	3.25 lin. ft.	.54	2.25 lin. ft.	.54	3.00 lin. ft.	.50	3.00 lin. ft.	.50	2.70 lin. ft.	1.45
Water[2]	2.50 lin. ft.	1.25	2.25 lin. ft.	1.13	3.00 lin. ft.	1.50	2.10 lin. ft.	1.05	2.25 lin. ft.	1.13
Planting and Seeding—(6½ sq. ft. grass @ .03, one tree every 60' @ $6.00)		.29		.29	See F'tnote 13	.49		.29		.29
Sub-Total		$8.42		$7.76		$9.73		$7.26		$8.13
For street improvements on which no houses face 15%		1.26		1.16		1.46		1.09		1.22
Engineering 6%		.58		.54		.67		.50		.56
Total		$10.26		$9.46		$11.86		$8.85		$9.91

[1] Storm drainage based on a minimum 15 inch pipe being constructed under one-third total linear feet of streets.
[2] In many areas the city or county participates in the cost of some of these items. This would reflect in a local cost sheet.
[3] Front foot cost based on a 26-foot pavement width using a 2-foot over-all width for curb and gutter, with the curb riser being 6 inches wide.
[4] Six inch Macadam or equal.
[5] One and one-half inch Asphaltic Concrete.
[6] Connecticut, Delaware, Massachusetts, Maryland, New Jersey, New York, Pennsylvania and Rhode Island.
[7] Alabama, Florida, Georgia, Kentucky, North Carolina, South Carolina, Tennessee and Virginia.
[8] Indiana, Illinois and Ohio.
[9] Arkansas, Colorado, Louisiana, Oklahoma, New Mexico, Texas and Wyoming.
[10] California, Oregon and Washington.
[11] Specifications for Base and Wearing Surface vary according to local materials and climate.
[12] 1947 prices on these items in Houston, Texas were found by Hugh Potter to be as follows: Grading $1.00 per cu. yd.; Curb and Gutter $1.60 per lin. ft. and Sidewalk $.35-40 per sq. ft.
[14] 6½ sq. ft. grass @ .05, one tree every 60' @ $10.00.
[15] Interest, liability insurance, social security, office overhead, etc., should be added to the above costs.

[13] Above estimates are based on development of a tract of about 30 acres. Current prices shown are reasonable for estimating purposes. Bids will vary from these figures depending on the contractor's volume of work in the area and its location with relation to delivery of material. Grading costs shown will be affected by extent to which shovel must be moved and by type of soil. Deeper and more consolidated cuts are cheaper than more shallow extended cuts.

Figure 16.

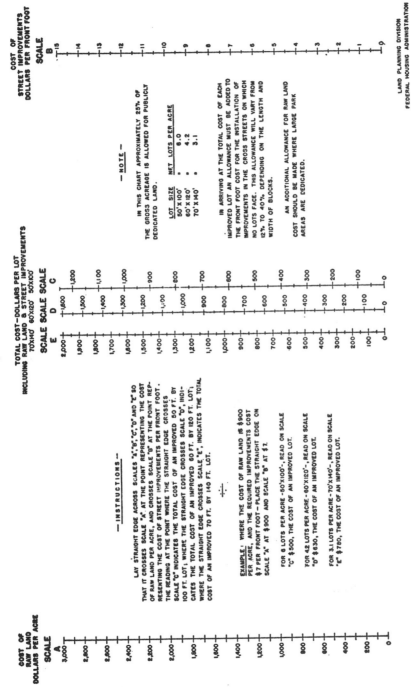

The approximate total cost of an improved lot can be computed on this chart from raw land costs and street improvement costs.

business. Additional off-street parking should always be provided on the church site.[1]

(c) It is the consensus of the Council that play areas are
needed in a residential community. However, considerable
difficulty has been experienced in managing and maintaining them. (See Part III.) The desirable size of a playground
varies with the population and composition of the neighborhood.
The following are minimum desirable sized playground areas for
various populations, exclusive of school sites:

Population	Size (acres)
2,000	3.25
3,000	4.00
4,000	5.00
5,000	6.00

Playgrounds of less than two to two and one-half acres are
of little value except for pre-school children's play lots. Five
per cent of the gross area of a project is considered about the
maximum amount of land a developer can afford to dedicate for
park and recreation purposes. Ideally located, a child should
have to walk no more than one-half mile to a playground.

A complete recreation area should be large enough to provide most of the following features:

A section for pre-school children.
Apparatus area for older children.
Open space for informal play.
Surfaced area for court games such as tennis, hand ball,
    shuffle board and volley ball.
Field for softball and mass games.
Area for story telling and quiet games.
Shelter house with toilet facilities.
Wading pool.
Corner for table games for older people.
Landscape features.

A good location for playgrounds is at or near the school site.
Some unsatisfactory experience with playgrounds has been van-

---

[1] Mr. Potter has stated, "I would not think of planning a large tract
without providing for several church sites. It gives a coordination to
families in the neighborhood, and aids in development of community
spirit. A church site should not be planned without sufficient off-street
parking around the church. This is sometimes neglected."

dalism in destruction of ornaments and equipment, and difficulty in selling adjacent houses. Adequate supervision should thus be assured either by the municipality, developer, or homes association if they are to be retained as assets to the development. The importance of this matter is reflected in the following resolution of the Council:

RESOLVED that the Community Builders' Council of the Urban Land Institute strongly favors the establishment of publicly or community dedicated children's playgrounds in connection with all residential development, and that insofar as possible, they should be combined with or contiguous to the school site in order that duplication of facilities will be avoided; and that such playground facilities will receive proper and continual supervision by the public authorities having such matters in charge.

(See Part III for problems of management.)

Interior block playgrounds are considered undesirable by a majority of the Community Builders' Council.[1] A few have found them satisfactory. It is generally felt, however, that the provision of playgrounds is a community obligation and that most of the unsatisfactory experience could be overcome by proper location as well as better supervision. Playground areas should be worked out in the initial stages with the planning commission and recreation, school or park board in order that they will fit into the city plan whether they are dedicated to the city or not.

(d) Noise and confusion in connection with outdoor swimming pools have been known to affect adversely the value of residences to a distance of 1300 feet. They must be properly located in public or private areas to overcome this objection. (See Part III.)

13. Landscape Planting.

A planting scheme should contribute to the beauty of a development and should serve a useful purpose as well. Undesirable

---

[1] Mr. Nichols' advice regarding this subject is worth noting: "In the Country Club District we dedicated and equipped several good 'interior-block playgrounds' at large cost to us. We had neighborhood objections to these playgrounds and are not now providing them. We believe playgrounds wherever possible should be provided in additional areas adjoining public schools. This reduces supervision cost, and combined facilities can be utilized. We believe in ample recreational areas, but I doubt that you can afford to contribute ten percent of your land as is often recommended. Then, too, small play areas are not usually needed in sections where you have large lots. We built public picnic ovens in some of our properties in the early days. Vandalism and unruly conduct of patrons of these ovens soon caused us to remove all of them."

views can be screened out and noise diverted by well located walls or screen plantings of shrubs and trees.

(a) *Existing Growth.* Existing trees on the development site should be saved whenever possible. A good tree may add greatly to the value of a lot. Road and building locations should be checked on the ground after staking, but before clearing the site. This permits changes in road location to save good trees. During construction, trees and roots should be protected from damage.

(b) *Street Trees.* Planting of street trees is ·a desirable, standard practice. Straight streets should have regularly planted trees except where building groups indicate different treatment. Narrow streets may have trees on one side only, preferably on the south or west side for effective shading. Long curves are most effective with trees on both sides or on the outside of the curve. Narrow streets, short streets, or those with one side higher than the other are best planted in an informal manner. Trees are commonly planted too close together. Fifty to sixty feet has been found better than 25 to 30 feet, depending on the variety and growing habits. See also page 66.

In higher priced developments splendid effects may be secured by plantings of single varieties of flowering trees such as hawthorn, dogwood, flowering crab, cherry, etc. During the flowering season they will attract hundreds of visitors and prospective buyers to the property.

(c) *Other Tree Planting.* In apartment groups, trees can be concentrated in groups at the ends of buildings, breaking long vistas and giving shade in contrast to sunny lawn areas. Low branched trees may be planted along back lot lines to reduce noise and give privacy to dwellings. Trees should be grouped in order to preserve as large open lawn areas as possible.

Good soil and drainage conditions are necessary for good tree growth. Where the existing conditions are unfavorable, use fewer trees but provide them with good soil and effective protection. It is always better to plant trees on a fill if well compacted and made with good soil than on a cut where the tree will be planted in subsoil.

Few varieties of trees already established will stand fills of more than a few inches over their roots or cuts which remove any substantial amount of the root system. In general, the spread of the root system can be roughly determined by the spread of the branches, although different species vary from this rule of thumb. Tree wells up to several feet in depth have sometimes been found satisfactory under favorable conditions. At best they can only serve to prevent fill against the trunk and for a limited radius around it. Fill around trees is always hazardous as the feeder roots which grow close to the surface must have air and drainage. Certain types of trees such as oaks and beech will practically always die if filled around. Before filling, a layer of coarse gravel or broken stone to the depth of 6″ to 8″ should be spread on the surface over the feeder roots. This assures air and drainage. A tree well built 6″ to a foot from the tree trunk and extending to the old ground level should be provided to keep the trunk from rotting. Vertical tiles are sometimes set at intervals above the feeder roots down to the level of the gravel or broken stone fill to provide additional air circulation.

(d) *Shrubs.* Shrubs and evergreens should be used in large masses only when required for practical reasons such as to prevent erosion on slopes or as a ground cover or a screen. Most shrubs should be planted as individual specimens or in small groups. Do not plant too close to buildings, and allow ample space along walks to permit normal growth without crowding. Shrubs or flower beds in the middle of lawn areas should be avoided. Use only hardy varieties. C. R. Walstrom, representing Chester Moores of Portland, Oregon, feels it is always wise to omit any high planting at street corners in order to avoid traffic accidents. Protective covenants should require future owners to remove any high planting which creates traffic hazards.

(e) *Protective Plantings.* Plantings of shrubbery and trees can be effectively used to screen out objectionable views and also to absorb and deflect noise.[1]

(f) *Hedges.* Hedges may be used in connection with play areas and at a few strategic points in the site plan, such as street

---

[1] An interesting solution to a serious problem in a development of houses costing up to $30,000 has been described by Irvin Blietz of Chicago. This project was adjacent to a railroad which ran close to the rear line of the lots in a cut. A very satisfactory screen was provided by an earth mound six feet high along the right-of-way, on top of which was placed a 6-foot cedar fence and heavy shrub planting. The fence and the shrubs screen the trains from view, and the sound vibrations are absorbed and deflected by the earth embankment. The slope of the bank was worked out so that air eddies were formed which control the drift of smoke.

corners where they must be kept low, and along project boundaries. Preference should be given to species that have an acceptable appearance without continuous trimming or pruning. In apartment projects low hedges along walks are effective in controlling foot traffic, and create a neat and harmonious appearance.

(g) *Vines.* Vines are usually easy to maintain and may be used liberally on masonry walls, especially blank end walls of buildings. Vines reduce noise and glare. However, they should not be used on frame construction due to the resulting damage to supports and buildings. Vines of various types are useful for ground cover in shady areas and to protect banks against erosion. Grass should seldom be planted on steep banks or terraces. Lists of plant materials are often misleading and do not take the place of advice from your landscape architect and nurseryman as to the best varieties for any particular local soil and climate.

C. STREET AND UTILITY CONSTRUCTION.

Following briefly are engineering considerations generally incorporated in the engineer's plans and specifications.

1. Project Grading Plans.

These plans consist of fixing approximate building floor elevations and finished grades for project streets, drives, walks, and other site areas. To be economical, plans should attain a reasonable balance of cut and fill, and avoidance of fills which will add to depth of building foundations. The existing ground level should be retained wherever possible near trees which are to be preserved. In general, lawns should slope toward streets or other surfaced areas which provide surface drainage directly into public streets. Earth banks should not exceed a 3 to 1 slope. Such slopes should be sodded or preferably planted with ground cover or shrubs. On long steep slopes sod should not be used because of difficulty of maintenance.

2. Surfaced Areas.

Selection of pavement types must be based upon a study of the nature of the subgrade, climatic conditions, comparative costs, probable wheel loads, character of project, and cost limitations. Street specifications should be such that they will be accepted in dedication by the municipality.

Bituminous bound paving is almost universally used by developers unless the municipality requires concrete. A good base reduces maintenance. The small extra cost of an 8-inch base compared to a 4 or 6-inch base is well worth the difference. A bituminous bound top course, either plant mixed or sprayed on hot, is common and satisfactory in practice. Where macadam or gravel pavement is used, a 6 to 8 inch rolled base with 1½ to 2-inch ready mixed or bituminous penetration top is standard practice in low cost projects.

To avoid glare and minimize unsightly discoloration from oil and grease on a concrete pavement, it is usually advisable to darken the surface with a light bituminous dressing, or to mix color compound, usually lamp black, with the concrete prior to placing.

There is objection to high road crowns. For bituminous bound roads ⅜ inches per foot is found to be satisfactory. This gives a 5-inch crown in a 26-foot roadway. Gravel roads require a higher crown, and on concrete roads a flatter crown is satisfactory.

Curbs and gutters are almost universally a necessary part of street construction. In very open estate development, however, it may be possible to utilize cobble stone or wide shallow grass gutters if slopes are favorable and proper maintenance is assured.

Sidewalks should generally be constructed of concrete. Gravel or cinder sub-base is not necessary for walks except under most unfavorable soil conditions. Steps in sidewalks should be avoided wherever possible, but stepped ramps may be permissible where slopes of over 15 per cent are encountered. If used, they should have a tread of not less than 5 feet to permit alternating the foot at each step, with a 5 to 6-inch riser. Where the sidewalk is laid along the curb, precaution should be taken against uneven settlement of the two elements. Sidewalks crossed by driveways to garages may require greater thickness or reinforcement, although this is not usually necessary if the subgrade is properly compacted.

3. Sewage Disposal.

Wherever possible public sewer systems should be used. The next choice is a community sewer system rather than individual disposal methods. Sewage disposal by septic tanks and tile fields for each dwelling should be resorted to only when absolutely necessary. Individual disposal will usually require an area of considerably larger dimensions than the normal suburban lot in order to provide for an adequate disposal field. However, this is not the only consideration. Sites for the disposal fields should slope away from the house, and should be kept free of trees and shrubbery both to insure action of sunlight and freedom from root growth which may clog the lines. The type of soil and sub-soil conditions will affect greatly both the area needed and the possibility of polluting nearby surface water or wells. The effluent from disposal fields located on hillsides has been found coming to the surface at considerable distances from the field where it originates. All of these considerations and others militate against the use of septic tanks. It is virtually impossible to adapt them to all of the varied conditions to be found within any given development. Even where conditions are favorable, the maintenance of individual septic tanks, after a few years use, frequently becomes a difficult problem. Where they must be used, be sure to call in the State Board of Health and be prepared to conduct percolation tests as these will have a direct bearing on the final lot dimensions required. Also bear in mind that disposal fields may have to be abandoned after some years and new fields provided.

Where the extension of public sewers is not possible, it is recommended that a small central community system be used. Several such systems have been developed in recent years and have been used in many community projects with considerable success. Among the companies which have developed this type of system are the Hays Process Company, Waco, Texas; Chicago Pump Company, Chicago, Illinois; Dorr Company, New York City; and the Pacific Flush Tank Company, New York City.

Where small private utility companies have been organized to operate these plants, they have proved more satisfactory than having them maintained by a property owners' association

The argument is often made that it is cheaper to install septic tanks rather than provide a central plant. This is true at today's costs if the question of initial cost of construction only is considered, as the cost of sewer connections, mains and plant has increased to a greater extent than that of septic tank installation. However, if all factors are considered, both the developer and the home owner may find they have lost money. As already mentioned, lot sizes must usually be greatly increased for the septic tank. This may mean that instead of providing a normal suburban lot ranging from 10,000 to 20,000 square feet or perhaps less, a lot of two to four times this amount will be required to provide for a septic tank and disposal field. Here market demand for acreage lots is involved, with relation to the cost of raw land and possible increase in other improvement costs including grading, water, streets, etc., stacked against the selling price of the lot. Within a relatively few years public sewers may be extended to the neighborhood and connections required in the interest of public health. In this event the cost of the septic tank installation is lost completely as lines are usually in the rear yard and cannot be converted. With a central system, however, the cost of laterals and house connections is not lost as they can usually be connected to the new sewer main without change. Thus the only loss to write-off is the treatment plant which may have some salvage value while septic tanks do not. If the typical 30-acre subdivision is used as an example, the net results of the two different systems would be about as follows:

With Septic Tank	With Central Plant
Maximum desirable density: one to two families/net acre; 24 to 48 families.	Desirable suburban density: four families/net acre; 120 families.
Septic tank installed __ $190/unit	Sewer mains _____ $112/unit
	House connections ____ 100/unit
	Plant prorated _____ 148/unit
Total for Septic tank __ $190/unit	Total for Central Plant $360/unit
Salvage with public connections _____ none	Salvage of mains and connections _____ $212/unit
	Plant—2% _____ 3/unit
Cost to be written off/unit _____ $190	$145

Contrary to popular opinion individual septic tanks require frequent attention and continued maintenance if they are to operate properly and avoid nuisance conditions. They should not be considered as other than temporary installations under even the most favorable conditions.

In planning your sewer system, the following points should be investigated carefully:

1. Is the existing system to which connections are to be made of adequate capacity? Is it a separate, or a combined sanitary and storm water system?

2. What is the basis upon which the city charges for the installation of sewers?

(a) Are they charged entirely to the developer?

(b) Is total or partial recovery of the initial cost possible?

(c) Can a special sewer improvement district be set up covering the area to be developed?

(d) How are costs allocated where mains and trunk lines must be constructed through the development to serve property beyond its borders?

3. Is a permit to discharge surface drainage into natural water courses required by the local or state government? Be sure to check this point as it may save you trouble and expense later.

In general the sewer lines should be located within street rights-of-way wherever possible but not necessarily under roadway paving. The system should be coordinated with other utilities and located to avoid existing trees.

The size of house connections to sewers should be not less than 6 inches to avoid clogging; all lateral sewers should not be less than 8 inches. Normally, sanitary sewers should not be laid in the same trench with water supply lines. However, it is possible in some cases, where permitted by the local authorities, to combine the lines in a double-shelf trench which will contain the sanitary sewer at the bottom and the water line on the shelf.

Surface drainage connections to sanitary sewer systems should generally be avoided.

4. Storm Sewers.

Except in open type of estate development, underground storm sewers will usually be required. Connection with the existing city system is always desirable. However, it is sometimes possible to retain certain natural drainage channels into which storm sewers can discharge, particularly if it is a perennial stream valley, which can be dedicated as a park. Check carefully the possibility of flooding during periods of heavy storm water discharge and establish park boundaries accordingly, bearing in mind that the development of upstream property as well as your own will greatly increase the rate of runoff from roofs, paved areas and open lawns.

5. Water Distributing System.

Mains should be located in the street, preferably in the park strip between walk and pavement, or where curb and sidewalk are contiguous, back of the sidewalk. Fire hydrants should be readily accessible, protected from traffic hazards, and located so as not to obstruct walks or parking.

A convenient rule of thumb in estimating the number of fire hydrants required is as follows: One hydrant per 400 to 500 feet of street, or approximately the square footage of the area of the property divided by 200,000. Where buildings are large, closely grouped, and inflammable, one hydrant per 300 to 400 feet is desirable.

As with sewers, a central water supply is always preferable to individual wells. As areas build up, individual wells become increasingly undependable both as to supply and water quality. Initial construction and subsequent maintenance of a central supply will usually be found less expensive and far more satisfactory. Many small private water companies are rendering satisfactory service.

In general, the same points as those listed under sewers should be checked including capacities and pressure of existing mains for both domestic service and fire protection, basis of municipal charges, and allocation of costs. The requirements for any new system should of course, be checked with the city, county and state authorities.

6. Pole Lines and Gas Service.

It is generally desirable to keep pole lines out of the street where they are unsightly and interfere with the trees, and to place them on easements along the rear lot line. In some areas public utility companies insist upon street location, and in some instances, due to topography and views, it may be desirable to locate them on streets. Poles placed on rear easements have proved highly satisfactory and are recommended in preference to street location as they are less unsightly and can be more readily screened by planting. Underground electric conduits are too expensive at the present time to consider except in very special cases. It is desirable to reserve a 10 foot easement, 5 feet on either side of the rear lot line for pole lines. Gas mains are usually placed in the street between pavement and sidewalk or between sidewalk and property line.

D. HOUSE PLANNING FOR OPERATIVE BUILDERS.

1. Floor Plans.

In a large project of low-cost houses, particular attention should be given to developing unit designs which take advantage of site, views, trees, and prevailing climatic conditions.

Fire insurance classifications and rates should be ascertained and units designed to obtain economical protection. They should also meet the FHA property and construction standards.

Where low-cost homes are built by one operator, the number of types of dwelling units or buildings should be kept to a minimum, but it is equally necessary that every effort be made to relieve the monotony of duplicated units. Varying setbacks from the street and the combined grouping of one and two-story houses can be successful in creating architectural interest. On this point Hugh Potter says: "Where the building sites are large and there are many trees or abundant planting of shrubs, we no longer restrict any street to either one or two-story houses." However, both J. C. Nichols and John Mowbray feel that greater architectural conformity is desirable.

Orientation of the house and interior room arrangement should be given careful consideration as they are affected by sun and prevailing winds.

Providing space in the attic for a future bedroom or bedrooms with roughed-in plumbing and heating has been found desirable in some instances.

Possible furniture placement should be carefully checked in its relation to electrical and heating outlets, windows and door swings. The better house you build, the less the maintenance will be. Elimination of moldings, fewer dust catchers, use of washable kitchen walls, and larger window panes, all reduce maintenance cost and have a definite sales incentive.

2. Heating and Cooling.

Radiant and solar heating is a new development which should be considered.[1]

---

[1] Hugh Russell has tried electric heating elements placed in the ceiling and has found them satisfactory.

Cooling equipment is being developed, but costs are too high as yet to make its use possible in any but high-priced homes.

3. Kitchen and Laundry Equipment.

There is a growing trend to equip houses not only with stoves and refrigerators, but also with dish washers, home laundries, clothes driers, and garbage disposal devices. Except for the fact that this additional equipment loads the price of a house, this trend may be desirable where real estate mortgages can include such equipment.

4. General.

(a) Low rambling or ranch type houses near high-priced two-story dwellings have been found objectionable in some areas in the north, not in others.

(b) Mixing of homes with kitchens on the street side next to homes with kitchens on the garden side is not considered objectionable. Where kitchens are on the front, it is recommended that the service entrance open on the side yard as there is objection to such entrances directly on the front. However, if you have alleys, check with the sanitation department on its collection requirements. It is not desirable to mix front and rear refuse collection in the same area.

(c) Rental housing should not be intermingled with single family houses for sale.

(d) It is recommended that storage space be provided in garages even where houses contain basements. Provision of storage space in the garage for tools, garden furniture, and similar articles is desirable. For single-car garages it has been found feasible to add 5 to 6 feet to the length of the garage for this purpose. This is preferable to widening the garage as this may require a greater lot width.

(e) In general, where garages are to be provided, the attached type is recommended. Although construction costs may be somewhat greater, offsetting savings may be effected in shorter driveways, integral construction, and width of lot permitted by the attached garage. The attached garage with direct access to the street is preferred to one placed on the side or rear, due to the great amount of paving required to maneuver a car in getting in and out. Garages in the rear yard detract greatly from its use for garden and outdoor living.

(f) Not many years ago porches were generally on the front of the house. With the increase in automobile and other street traffic they were moved to the side, and now have completed the movement to the rear or garden side of the house where they are better related to pleasant living and afford a much greater degree of privacy.

PART III

Protecting the Future of the Development

A. PROTECTIVE COVENANTS.

1. General.

Protective covenants, sometimes called private deed restrictions, have been found from many years of experience to be an essential instrument in maintaining stability, permanence, character, and desirability in community development. They are not to be considered as taking the place of public regulations such as zoning. Both types of regulation are essential, and are not necessarily overlapping. Zoning provides for certain limited regulations which are considered the minimum necessary in the interests of public health, safety, and general welfare. Protective covenants are contracts between private parties which usually go beyond the regulations enforceable by public authorities in protecting the amenities inherent or built into any particular type of community development.

Protective covenants for any given development should take the form of blanket provisions which apply to the whole area rather than separate covenants in each deed. Basic restrictions should be made a part of the recorded plat. If, in addition, certain further special provisions are found to be necessary for any particular properties, they should be added to the individual deeds between developer and purchaser. Covenants should be drafted by a person thoroughly qualified in this particular field. Some attorneys specialize in this work and should be retained to pass on the legal aspects. However, the details of the requirements and protection to be provided should be worked out in collaboration with the developer and the land planning consultant. The covenants recommended by the F.H.A. have been used satisfactorily in thousands of subdivisions and have been approved by the title and large mortgage investment institutions. They should be considered as minima, particularly in high-priced property where more detailed controls are usually desirable.

2. Specific Controls.

The following list contains the customary and recommended provisions to be found in blanket covenants: (See Appendix for recommended forms)

(a) Control of land use, including restrictions as to type and design of dwellings.

(b) Architectural control of all structures including fences and walls. Some developers retain control over the house color. This is particularly important in group or attached houses.

(c) Minimum sideyard and setback regulations, including location or prohibition of accessory buildings.

(d) Control of minimum lot size.

(e) Prohibition of nuisances, and regulation of "for sale" or other signs.

(f) Restriction of temporary dwellings.

(g) Limitation of size of structure through a minimum cost or area clause, or both. The inclusion of cost restrictions is debatable, particularly in a period of increasing or irregular construction costs. Where such a restriction is included, it may be advisable to relate the required minimum cost to an authoritative price index such as the United States Bureau of Labor Commodity Index. This has been done by David Bohannon in California. Probably the most simple and effective method is the specification of a certain minimum habitable floor area exclusive of garages and basements. Such a restriction is capable of direct interpretation, is less open to controversy, and can be used alone or in conjunction with a minimum cost limitation if necessary. Some developers depend entirely on architectural control for maintaining standards of cost, size, and character.

(h) Reservation for utility easements; usually five feet on either side of the rear or side lot line.

(i) Other clauses which may be found desirable or necessary can be added to the above depending on local custom, character of the development, and type of market. Many developers control the grading plan of individual lots, the elevations of first floor building levels, and location of drives and garages.

3. Effective Period.

Some covenants are drawn up with a definite termination date, but opinion favors covenants which run with the land, subject to revision by a stipulated percentage, (not less than a majority) of the property owners at the end of a 25 to 40-year period, and with provisions for automatic extension in the event no action is taken by the owners at the time specified. It is recommended that any action to be taken by the owners should be required to precede the termination date by at least 5 years. This permits considered action and prevents pressure being brought to bear by any individual who might benefit by an immediate change. No one should have the right to remove general covenants before the end of the minimum period. However, some developers insert provisions retaining minor rights of deviation within certain limits, such as building line adjustment.

4. Enforcement.

Unless adequate machinery is set up initially for proper enforcement, covenants may become ineffective through non-observance and violation. It is always advisable to provide for the establishment of an organization which will take over this duty as one of its functions. Control by the developer of the affairs of such an organization should be passed on to the residents as rapidly as possible. One exception to this is to be found in the enforcement of architectural control which should normally be retained by the developer as long as he has a stake in the community. The establishment of a proper community organization is discussed in the following section under Homes Associations.

In evaluating the type and extent of the protective covenants which should be placed on any particular development, J. C. Nichols says: "Don't make the mistake of placing restrictions on too large areas in advance of knowing your demand. This may result in some land carrying higher restrictions than later demand will justify. If you use minimum cost restrictions, we recommend a lower general base restriction on a subdivision, adding additional cost restrictions as may be justified when individual sales are made and areas become established. with higher cost homes. Always, of course, you should retain approval of architectural design of all structures, including fences, walls, etc. Some developers depend wholly on architectural control and do not set up minimum costs, and perhaps this is a better method.

"In the early days of the J. C. Nichols Company we made the mistake of restricting land only as it was sold. Today we file a restriction on each area as it is platted subjecting all the land therein to our basic restrictions (setting forth any areas reserved for shops, schools, churches, etc.). Everyone who buys in such a subdivision has an injunction right against any violation of restriction. We do not believe it is fair for a developer to place individual restrictions on each lot as it is sold, and not commit the balance of his unsold land."

B. MAINTENANCE AND HOMES ASSOCIATIONS.

1. Successful Associations.

Among the homes associations which have been outstandingly successful are those found in the Country Club District of Kansas City; the Roland Park developments of Baltimore; St. Francis Wood, San Francisco; San Lorenzo Village, Alameda County, California; Forest Hills Gardens, Long Island, New York; and Park Hills, Berkeley, California.

Procedures for the establishment and operation of homes associations have been set forth by the various developers in more or less detail depending on the type of community, price range, and presence of municipal services.

Briefly, the methods generally accepted in setting up an association in a new community are as follows:

The development company initially is the owner of all property within the development. It proceeds to set up the association as part of the covenants or under articles of incorporation executed by the company, in which the company or five to seven persons (usually company officials) are named to act temporarily as directors or officers until their successors are elected. These successors should be resident owners of property within the area covered by the covenants. The association should have a charter from the state to operate as a maintenance organization.

2. Powers and Duties.

These articles set forth the purposes and duties of the association which may include:

(a) Maintenance of streets, parks, and other open spaces until such activity is taken over by public authority or in lieu thereof.

(b) Maintenance of vacant, unimproved and unkempt lots.

(c) Refuse collection, street sweeping, snow removal, police and fire protection, and maintenance of water and sewer mains and sewage disposal systems until taken over by public authority or in lieu thereof.

(d) Payment of taxes and assessments, if necessary, on all property held by the association for general use of the community.

(e) Approval of architectural and site plans for new construction. Most developers have found it better to retain control over architectural design, planting, etc., during the active development period. In some cases this function has been turned over to an "Art Jury", membership of which is determined by the company. This method probably insures a more consistent degree of good design than by giving the functions to the homes association, the members of which may be swayed by special interest in the purchase or in the effect which the new house will have on their particular property. Control over this function may be assigned to the homes association after almost all land has been sold by the developer.

(f) Enforcement of private covenants and restrictions.

(g) Determination and collection of annual charges or assessments, which become liens against property in event of non-payment. In this connection the Council urges the importance of filing the covenants prior to the sale of lots in order that they may be a prior lien over any later mortgages.

(h) Dispersal of funds collected for maintenance, taxes, or other proper charges levied against property of the association.

(i) Acquisition or disposal of property in the interests of the association, either by purchase, sale, or dedication to a public authority.

(j) Borrowing of money for the proper conduct of its affairs.

(k) Performance of other proper functions in the interest of the association and the community such as maintenance and replacement of street trees, erection of street signs, operation of a community information office, etc.

In drafting the organizational set-up of the homes association, J. C. Nichols has this to say:

"In our early charters we made the serious mistake of limiting the total tax per square foot, and some associations cannot levy over a mill per square foot under their charters. Others have the right by a vote of the majority of the owners attending a meeting called for that purpose to raise it to a total not to exceed two mills. With our present day high costs, the associations with the limitation are in grave difficulty, and several of them are trying to meet the situation by asking for voluntary additional annual contributions to the homes association. This results in a few of the owners refusing to pay; consequently, a number of our associations have had to give up some of their essential duties. I do not believe it will slow down sales to have the charter provide that the assessments can be increased by a vote of the majority of owners attending a meeting called for that purpose, and I certainly should not require that it has to be a majority of all home owners.

"In our association the man owning a big tract has no more votes than a man owning a small tract except that the small tract owners must comply with the minimum lot width permitted. In other words, a man could not divide a lot up into several small ownerships and get additional votes. And, even though our company might still own half the land in a subdivision, we only have one vote. This has worked all right over some forty years."

3. Resident Control.

Rules and regulations as to the number of directors, eligibility and voting power of members, and modification of the by-laws are set forth. Membership is usually limited to resident owners and persons purchasing a home site for their personal use. Voting power can be determined by the association or can be based on the number of square feet of land held or contracted for, or upon the number of building sites so held with a corresponding pro-rated interest in all property held by the association. The latter method provides an orderly relinquishment of control over the community to the home owners themselves. This is a highly desirable objective. Experience has shown that those associations have been most successful which have had community responsibility turned over to the residents as rapidly as possib' with the minimum of control retained by the development company except in the early stages. In some cases the incorporation of the association is left to the discretion of the members. However, incorporation is desirable especially where public services are being performed and power is given to collect and disburse money.

By-laws governing the association which provide the usual specifications as to membership, voting rights, property rights, corporate powers, elections, powers and duties of directors and other officers, conduct of meetings, and amendments may also be established initially by the company, although this may be left to the association to develop.

It has been found that an association comprised of between 500 and 750 families is large enough to operate financially and small enough to retain a close neighborhood interest.

4. Maintenance and Operation.

Some developers have established contractual relations with the association whereby they furnish the maintenance and community services. This method has the advantage of relieving the association of operational details, and the developer, being directly concerned as a partner in the welfare of the community, will usually furnish better service at less cost then would some concern with no direct interest.

Several large community builders have retained control of maintenance and assessment collections in lieu of setting up a homes association. While this method is used successfully and has certain advantages in insuring consistent maintenance of the community assets, it does not provide the degree of resident participation which seems desirable and makes it difficult in the future for the developer to divest himself of these responsibilities should he desire to do so. Ability to assign these functions should always be insured.

Instead of a homes association, River Oaks (Hugh Potter's development in Houston) has a maintenance fund provision in each deed which levies an assessment of not to exceed two mills per square foot upon all site owners, including the River Oaks Corporation itself on the sites it still owns. The River Oaks Corporation acts as Trustee in the collection and disbursement of the funds. The operation of the maintenance work is under the direct supervision of a capable engineer. Many highly desirable services are rendered to the residents of River Oaks under this maintenance fund at a surprisingly low cost.

5. Recreation Areas and Clubs.

One of the greatest assets which a community development can provide is recreation facilities for the younger generation of the community. The modus operandi for providing these facilities should rest initially with the developer. Relinquishment to the residents should, however, be insured at the earliest moment. Ownership and operation of the recreation areas may be part of the homes association's activities or might be separate therefrom.

An excellent example of how such an organization may be set up and operated as a club is to be found in the experience of a development located in western United States. The community consisted of between 400 and 500 medium priced home sites of which about 25 per cent were developed at the time the club was established. Several tracts of land amounting to approximately 15 acres, and including several stream valley parks, a waterfront, and a club house site, were deeded by the developer to the club which had been previously incorporated.

The developer also constructed a complete club house building which was to be furnished and equipped by the members, and two concrete tennis courts which could be used for various activities throughout the year including ice skating, outdoor dancing, etc. Total costs involved including the land, tennis courts, club house, fencing, site improvement, and incidental expenses including incorporation amounted to approximately $65 per lot. Expenses of club operation during its first year (1940) were approximately $1,000 of which almost 30 per cent went for street lighting throughout the community. Membership dues, originally set up at $24.00 per year per family, were subsequently determined to be about one-half that amount and have been on this basis ever since. The development is now completely sold and will thus be able to operate on a budget about five times as great as that originally established with no increase in family dues.

Provision of facilities such as those described above will often cost the developer no more than an extensive advertising and publicity campaign, and will create a sustained value which will continue to pay dividends for many years in the future.

Developers have, in some cases, spent large sums to provide golf courses and similar facilities which have not provided for the juvenile population. The reason why most persons purchase a home is to raise a family in the right environment and to offer them all advantages within their means. Not to recognize this fact is a common mistake in many developments.

While initial establishment of homes associations, clubs, or both, is highly desirable, it is possible in many cases to organize such groups in already developed communities. Experience also shows that this type of organization is not peculiar to high cost developments. It could form the working basis for any community development and can be adapted to meet particular conditions. Many associations also function as a social nucleus in sponsoring community functions, events, and celebrations. It provides a framework for collective effort within the neighborhood which is often very difficult to obtain effectively.

The value of homes associations in community development is indicated in the following statement by J. C. Nichols: "We made the mistake in not setting up homes associations in our properties in the Country Club District at the very beginning, with power to assess 'land' for neighborhood service. We now have 19 such associations, all functioning in an excellent manner under one common staff, and every lot is sold subject to a land assessment for such associations. We even subject our unsold land, where street improvements are in, to this tax. (This tax is not on improvements.) These associations create neighborhood responsibility through the years, supply many needs and services, and go far to maintain values.

"Homes associations can be of great value in enforcing protective covenants, and in working with public officials.

"The question of care of vacant lots in a subdivision can be solved by an effective homes association with real powers. Be sure to give your homes association broad powers to meet all future and changing needs."

C. SELLING THE PROJECT.

1. Desirability.

In addition to the establishment of a normal sales organization, various incentive methods have been found successful in selling homes and home sites. Various Council members have suggested the following ideas as methods which they have used to advantage:

(a) So that the customers could sell themselves, maps designating the lots and prices have been given to them allowing them to find the various lots with the help of plainly marked signs.

(b) Lots difficult to sell have been offered on anniversary sales at price reductions. Buyers could pay as little as 10 per cent down with 5 per cent interest, and with not more than 30 per cent of the total payment made in any one year.

(c) Libraries of magazines and books on house and garden architecture have been made available and used effectively in stimulating interest of prospective home buyers.

(d) Builders of the first group of houses in a development have been given bonus certificates representing cash amounts.

(e) A colored rendering of his home has been given the buyer for display to his friends and acquaintances.

(f) Display rooms of building materials may be effective. They should be set up to indicate the soundness of construction and the choice of design and materials which are available to the prospective buyers. Unfortunately, this method is costly to maintain and difficult to keep up to date and has not been found successful by a number of Council members under present conditions.

(g) The poorest lots should be built on first by the developer. A much greater return can thus be secured and sales stimulated in the less desirable areas.

On this point J. C. Nichols offers the following advice: "Don't make the mistake of building homes on your best lots in a new subdivision to get it started. We believe it is wise to build such first homes on the areas difficult to sell as vacant lots. Try to make your poorest property the best in your subdivision. Be sure to maintain signs on all property reserved for shops, churches, schools, etc. This may save you a lot of grief."

(h) Leaving a vacant lot between houses has been found successful by a few developers in some instances but is not generally recommended.

(i) On higher priced property it has been found desirable to provide a reasonable amount of planting on vacant lots avoiding, however, planting on the area to be occupied by the building.

(j) As incentives, salesmen have been helped to build their own homes by being given architectural services and a lot at cost.

(k) Prizes, bonuses, or other incentives to salesmen have proved good practice.

(l) Sales commissions can be based on a sliding scale percentage which increases with the amount, volume, length of service, or combinations of these.

(m) Weekly reports should be required from salesmen at sales meetings to keep them on their toes.

(n) Where the sales organization is large, systems of cards can be developed showing all business that can be done with a client such as insurance, loans, legal work, house and lot sale, and appraisals. Individual cards can thus be sent to various sales departments for follow-up.

A word of warning in counting on future profits is sounded by J. C. Nichols: "Do not figure future estimated profits on unsold land. This has broken many a developer. Be sure to charge off to each year's operating cost all interest, all taxes, all maintenance on unsold land,—the developer who does not compound interest against himself for such charges is a poor businessman. A lot of developers overlook compounding of interest on all such items."

2. Modernizing Old Subdivisions and "Shopworn" Lots.

Various methods have been employed to modernize old subdivisions. They include:

(a) Removal of high and overgrown planting, and replanting.

(b) Building new houses for sale on vacant lots.

(c) Sale of vacant lots to adjoining property owners.

(d) Purchase, repainting and modernizing of some of the older houses will help to bring back values.

(e) Retention of vacant lots for much over five years is normally a losing proposition because of maintenance and taxes. Dispose of them.

(f) Provision of small parks and playgrounds.

(g) Resubdividing of groups of lots along modern lines where possible.

(h) Removal of obsolete restrictions which are non-terminating, through court procedure.

(i) Furnish paint to the owner of a shabby house if he will agree to clean up and put his property in attractive shape.

(j) Group meetings of the home owners to stimulate new interest and encourage friends to come into the area.

Charles Joern of La Grange, Illinois, feels that developers have given too little attention to the possibilities of redeveloping old subdivisions and shopworn lots, especially in the field of assembling tax delinquent property.

PART IV
Planning and Management of Shopping Centers

A. SIZE AND LOCATION.

1. Estimating Size.

The determination of the immediate and ultimate size of a shopping center is a matter which should be given very careful and detailed study. It is generally agreed that on the average a minimum of 500 families will be needed to support a center of ten to twelve shops, and 1,000 to 3,000 families to support twenty-five to forty shops. However, this number will vary considerably with the scale of income of the families tributary to the center, proximity and character of competing areas, type and living habits of the population served, and similar factors.

The importance of highway approaches from other areas and the transportation serving the center should be stressed. Shopping centers will frequently draw a sizable portion of their volume from areas outside of what might be considered the normal tributary or trading area. The greater increase of population in outlying areas, which is expected to result from urban freeway construction into the central city area, will undoubtedly bring about a greater growth of outlying business centers.

Several methods have been developed for estimating the amount of area needed for shops. While various refinements have been made, the basic methods are as follows:

(a) Linear feet of store frontage per 100 persons. This was an early method of developing norms from the amount of business frontage actually in use in an urban area. It has been applied in a large number of cities and has produced relatively uniform results. Harland Bartholomew, for instance, found in 1932 around 64 linear feet of commercial frontage per 100 persons in sixteen self-contained cities he studied of which 28 feet was in the central city and 36 feet in the remainder. Later checks made in 1940 revealed an increase from 63.7 to 78.6 in the same cities. The reliability of this method has decreased in recent years as the greater use of parking stations, and the greater store widths and depths demanded by super markets and similar type stores tend to affect the validity of the results. It is useful primarily for city-wide land use surveys.

97

Table 8.

Consumer Expenditures
Average Expenditures of American Families for Main Categories of Consumption, by Income Level, 1935-36

Average Expenditure Per Family For:

Income Level	All Items	Food	Housing	Household Operation	Clothing	Automobile	Medical Care	Recreation	Furnishings	Personal Care	Tobacco	Education	Transportation other than auto	Reading	Other Items
$ 2,000 – $ 2,500	1,968	617	349	213	207	200	91	62	76	42	38	20	22	20	11
$ 2,500 – $ 3,000	2,302	690	404	260	255	242	109	81	84	49	41	30	24	22	11
$ 3,000 – $ 4,000	2,729	770	485	319	316	289	132	105	102	54	48	37	31	27	14
$ 4,000 – $ 5,000	3,276	852	571	400	408	382	158	136	110	66	53	57	35	31	17
$ 5,000 – $10,000	4,454	1,038	784	584	557	522	248	206	158	89	62	83	48	41	34
$10,000 – $15,000	6,097	1,214	1,204	761	829	681	227	340	227	114	79	227	114	57	23

From: Consumer Expenditures in the United States, National Resources Planning Committee, 1939.
(These figures should be considered only as guides.)

98

(b) Square feet of store per 100 persons. This method avoids the objection made to the lineal method, but like the lineal method is not particularly adaptable to use for individual projects. A large number of successful shopping centers has been found to contain an average area of about 4,000 square feet per 100 persons living in the tributary area.

(c) Rational method. This method is based on the determination of the number and type of retail outlets which can operate successfully with relation to the needs and buying power of the population in a given area. Approximations can be obtained by the use of tables similar to those shown in Table 8 and Appendices E to I. The number of tributary families times their normal yearly expenditures for various items will provide a guide to the approximate sales volume which may be expected.

This kind of study is adapted to individual projects and can be further refined and extended with the availability of additional local data. David Bohannon has used a detailed form of this method in evaluating a shopping center location which he is developing and which illustrates the kind of survey warranted in the larger center. The economic aspects of the survey were prepared by McConnell's Economic Surveys and cover the following items:

1. Determination of the Economic Trading Area Tributary to the Shopping Center.

2. Present Population, Families, and Purchasing Power for:
(a) The entire county.
(b) The trading area.
(c) Ratio of trading area to county.

3. Population, Families, and Purchasing Power for the Trading Area Estimated for 1950.

4. Annual Purchasing Power after Deducting Other Expenditures of:
(a) Federal taxes.
(b) Automobile transportation costs.
(c) Mortgages and rentals.
(d) Local taxes.
(e) Insurance, savings, etc.
(f) Retail sales in other centers within the economic area.

99

Deducting items (a) through (f) from the gross purchasing power leaves the commodity dollars spent elsewhere.

5. Analysis of Competitive Retail Shopping Areas.

6. Analysis of the Proposed Shopping Center regarding Type of Stores and the Priority of Their Establishment in the Center.

An item of interest is the stress which has been laid on provision for parking. The center as now designed provides for all the automobiles in the tributary area to park on the average of three times a week assuming a five-hour shopping day. This is considered a nearly ideal ratio.

Hugh Russell has used the so-called "minute drive theory" in developing data on tributary population and sales volume. This method is adaptable to outlying centers where local public transportation within the tributary area is not available. Briefly, it contemplates basing the area to be served by the center on that area that is within a certain number of minutes driving time of the site. As in other methods, the time chosen will depend upon the location and nature of competing centers.

In the above discussion it should not be assumed that the Council is advocating the accelerated decentralization of business. Rather, it recognizes the importance of maintaining a strong and healthy central business district in every city which should continue as the financial and office building center and as the location for the principal stores serving the entire urban and suburban area. The Council recognizes, however, that the central business districts, especially in our larger cities, as now developed and constituted, cannot possibly serve all of the business needs of the urban area either from the standpoint of accommodating the trade, or of the resulting traffic which would be generated. In this discussion of shopping centers, the Council envisions a well-rounded city with the main business district located in the central area, with good transportation facilities leading to and from the various parts of the city, and with a reasonable number of outlying community shopping centers designed to best serve the needs of the nearby residential development.

Plate VII. Panorama of the Early Part of the Country Club Plaza. Kansas City, Missouri.

2. Acquiring Land.

Where there is fair possibility for growth, sufficient area should be acquired for expansion and for control. However, no more shops should be constructed than are needed at the time. Where a shopping center has made a success, it has been the experience that some one else will build shops adjacent if land is available and the zoning ordinance will allow the use. The possibility that land zoned for residential uses across the street from a shopping center may be changed to permit business use is always present and should be considered. E. L. Ostendorf of Cleveland emphasizes that you can afford to buy extra land for shopping centers in order to protect it from undesirable encroachment and competition, and especially to provide for the rapidly increasing number of automobiles per thousand population. If you do not have control of the stores across the street, your tenants may be placed at a disadvantage by unbalanced grouping of store types, signs, advertising methods, preemption of parking areas, and similar factors which will be reflected in their sales and thus in the prosperity of the center as a whole.

3. Location.

Within the community area zoned for business, the location of a shopping center is the problem of the developer. The closest cooperation is suggested with all municipal or county officials. Always remember, you can't put a successful shopping center at just any street intersection.

In new subdivisions the location for the shopping center should be selected before the street plan of the area is determined. Size and location should be based upon a survey of existing and possible future competing centers, and a recognition of possible trade shifts. Your zoning map will indicate existing and potential competing areas. Modern zoning practice is toward localized business islands rather than string development.

Zoning ordinances in many cities do not provide for parking stations except as a commercial use in common with other uses permitted in business districts. This acts as a deterrent to providing off-street parking space and provides no insurance of permanency. In order to secure adequate and well located park-

Plate VIII. A Pioneer in Modern Design.
        Shopping Center, Houston, Texas,
        River Oaks Corporation, Hugh Potter, President.

ing facilities, it is recommended that cities establish regulations whereby off-street parking stations may be provided in areas adjacent to shopping centers which will both serve the center and create buffer areas between business and residential uses. Several methods have been devised to provide for this intermediate use. Probably the most common method is to permit residential land to be used for parking which is contiguous to or across the street from a commercial district under certain specified conditions including proper approaches, screening and lighting designed to protect adjacent residential uses. This is usually handled by the Board of Appeals or Adjustment as a special exception or permit procedure rather than as an amendment to the zoning map. The creation of a parking district as a zoning use district may be questioned on legal grounds as it creates a special one purpose district. Court decisions on the legality of this type of regulation should probably be sought before it is recommended. However, the Council believes that Zoning Boards of Appeal should be liberal in granting special exceptions for automobile parking where relief is needed, not only to provide additional parking but to relieve traffic congestion on the streets.

The trend for parking to be considered as a public use is reflected in the fact that 33 states have passed legislation permitting municipalities to undertake the provision of off-street parking in one form or other as a municipal function.[1] While most of this is directed at the downtown problems, municipal action in this field is not necessarily limited to the central business district.

Lacking other more definite guides, a good rule of thumb is to anticipate other local business islands within ½ to 1 mile, if not under your control, depending on the income groups and type of development. In higher cost more open development, where a greater use of the automobile and of telephone ordering is common, centers should be one mile or more apart.

Shopping centers should be approximately one mile apart in single family residential areas. Transportation, multiple housing, income grouping, and the relation and type of other centers, all enter into the problem of location, as well as the size of the center.

As level land as possible should be chosen for a shopping center site. Grades increase construction and maintenance costs and make planning less flexible and usually less satisfactory.

---

[1] Parking Manual, American Automobile Association, Washington 6, D. C., 1946.

If topography is hilly, it is usually better to locate the shopping center at the bottom rather than at the top of a grade.

The shopping area should be so located that the street plan leads into it from the tributary areas. Close proximity to main thoroughfares is highly desirable.

Walter Schmidt, Cincinnati, makes the following recommendation regarding business locations: "The side of the street upon which the small shopping center should be located will depend on the habits of the prospective shoppers. Where the shopping is done largely by the 'going-home' crowd, the right side of the street outbound is preferable. This is not universally true, however. Many centers are located out a considerable distance and the shopping is done by the housewife. If the center lies cityward of the tributary population, it should probably be located on the right side of the street city-bound. Each case should be determined individually. Larger centers will, of course, occupy both sides of the street."

One-way streets should never be designed into a shopping center. While they are used effectively as an expedient traffic device in central areas, they are not desirable from a shopping and merchandising standpoint and should be discouraged. Locations directly on major thoroughfares carrying high speed traffic are desirable only when adequate provision is made for safe and convenient access to parking off the travelled way.

B. SITE PLANNING FOR SHOPPING CENTERS.

1. Buffer Area.

The need for physical buffers such as parks, playgrounds, churches, public buildings, and multiple housing between shopping and adjacent single family residential areas is emphasized by E. L. Ostendorf.

Where such buffers are not possible, the use of walls, solid fences or narrow but dense plantings of hedge or evergreen material should be provided. Failure to insure permanent and effective physical separations between business and single family residential uses will detract greatly from the value and desirability of the latter.

2. Blocks.

While long blocks are desirable in residential development, the opposite is true for shopping centers. Blocks of 400 to 600 feet in length are generally recommended as the shorter block produces more corner locations and creates shorter distances around blocks. "Massed" shopping areas are always preferable to "string" street development. Hugh Potter has found it desirable to divide a 600 foot block into two blocks.

3. Streets.

(a) *Roadways.* In shopping areas the minimum width of roadway with diagonal parking at both curbs is 70 feet with three lanes of moving traffic. A 60-foot roadway is minimum width for parallel parking or for parallel parking on one side and diagonal parking on the other. Where streets are dedicated, do not count too much on the continued use of curb parking in lieu of providing your own off the street, especially on major thoroughfare routes. Too great a corner curb radius increases street width at pedestrian crossings, decreases curb parking space, and encourages increased car speeds at corners. A radius of not more than fifteen feet has been found desirable in shopping centers. Divided roadways except on major streets or at intersections are not recommended. Pedestrian safety islands, particularly at wide intersections with 60 feet or more of paving, are recommended. These should be designed to channelize automobile traffic and provide pedestrian safety at crossings. Islands should be of sufficient length and not too high or pedestrians will walk around them. Six inches is a maximum height. Painting will increase their visibility. Safety islands on either side of the pedestrian crossing have proved successful, as they give protection to the pedestrian, help to channelize the crosswalk, and remove the need for stepping up and down.

Curbs at intersections should not be over six or seven inches high unless there is danger of street flooding.

(b) *Alleys.* According to James Britton of Greenfield, Massachusetts, the desirable width for alleys is 20 feet. A greater width invites employee parking, and a narrower width makes it difficult for large trucks to pass or maneuver. Concrete curbs and corners of buildings at alley entrances should be protected by iron bands or other structural member. Caution should be exercised in dedicating alleys to the city because of possible future need to change or use the alley space. Easements for utilities may be necessary if alleys are not dedicated. Short, dead-end alleys are being used successfully in some centers, thereby

Plate IX. Inside the Rear Service Court.

HIGHLAND PARK SHOPPING VILLAGE, Dallas, Texas. Hugh E. Prather.

Plate X. Outside the Rear Service Court.
HIGHLAND PARK SHOPPING VILLAGE, Dallas, Texas.

eliminating a break in store frontage and increasing the amount of frontage on one street.

Interior loading courts or other forms of off-street loading platforms should always be provided for deliveries of merchandise. These may take the form of a central facility to serve all of the stores, or of individual facilities for certain types of stores requiring frequent service and volume deliveries.

(c) *Sidewalks.* For principal shopping streets in larger centers, a 17-foot sidewalk width is considered the minimum to provide for fire hydrants, mail boxes, street signs, street lights, trash receptacles, street trees, and free pedestrian movement. Side street walks may be 12 to 15 feet wide. The use of street trees requires these widths as minimum.

(d) *Street Trees.* Trees are considered desirable in outlying shopping centers by most operators, particularly in the south. For street planting they should be high branching, of a clean variety and able to withstand adverse soil conditions. They should be planted not less than 50 feet apart. If low branched, they obstruct view of store windows and for this reason are sometimes objectionable. Such street trees lessen neighborhood objection from nearby homes.

(e) *Pole Lines.* Public service lines and poles should not be placed in the streets of shopping centers. They are ugly, and dangerous in sleet storms. These should be located in the alleys with lines underground at street crossings, or placed entirely underground if possible. However, underground installation costs have become almost prohibitive in recent years, being estimated as high as 10 times that of overhead lines in some areas.

4. Parking Stations.

(a) *Size.* The provision of off-street parking as an integral part of shopping centers has become a major and not an incidental consideration. From an area standpoint parking stations now consume more space than all other features combined. Careful study must be given, however, to each individual project as the considerations of its ultimate size, location with relation to public transportation, type and income level of the tributary population, and local shopping habits and characteristics will all affect the final decision.

Over a long period of experimentation and experience with the operation of parking stations in connection with shopping centers, the members of the Council recommend that, under average conditions, two square feet of off-street space should be permanently reserved for parking for each square foot of store area provided. Where the amount of "walk-in" trade is expected to be relatively high because of adjacent multi-family development or relatively low income groups, this ratio may be lowered somewhat. Where drive-in trade will form the bulk of the patronage, ratios up to three to one are now used. Examples of this are to be found in recent projects developed by Council members. David Bohannon is providing two to one parking in the 40-acre Hillsdale Center, San Mateo, California, exclusive of curb space which increases the parking space about 30 per cent. Hugh Russell, after a survey of shopping centers throughout the country, is using the same ratios in a thirty acre center now under development. Waverly Taylor in studying the parking needs for a smaller park and shop center in Washington, D. C., found that a two to one parking ratio was a desirable minimum even where 60 per cent of the patronage was walk-in trade.

J. C. Nichols has found the one to one parking ratio used in his Plaza development to be inadequate, and is at great cost buying back land previously sold in order to increase his parking. It is worth noting that the Country Club Plaza has 54 per cent of its area in streets compared with 25 per cent in the central business district. One of the major difficulties encountered in the larger centers is employee parking. In one of his larger centers Mr. Nichols found over 700 employees' cars occupying off-street parking space for an eight-hour period. If these were eliminated, a turn-over of five to eight cars per day could be expected providing space for 3,500 to 5,600 drive-in customers. Remedies for this situation include lease clauses prohibiting employee parking in customer lots, or at street curbs, provision of employee lots in less central locations, and opening the parking area only after working hours have started. In cases where apartment occupants preempt commercial parking space, the prohibition of all night parking should be enforced. Multi-family development should provide its own adequate parking areas.

Plate XI. Hot Spot of the Country Club Plaza, Kansas City, Missouri.
Over 50,000 cars pass through this intersection daily without traffic control lights.

Figure 17. Plan of Naylor Road Shopping Center, Washington, D. C.

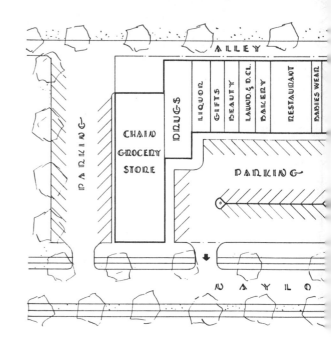

Plate XII. Taking Advantage of a Sloping Site.
NAYLOR ROAD SHOPPING CENTER, Washington, D. C. Waverly Taylor, In

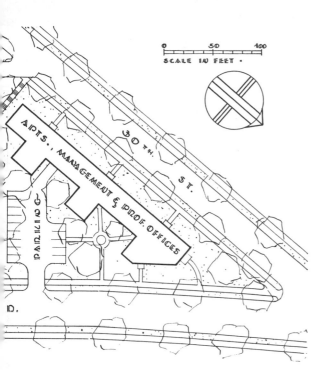

A three-hour parking limit is recommended for shopping center stations. While the provision of free parking in outlying centers is desirable and should be continued as long as possible, the developer would be wise not to enter into agreements with tenants which would tie his hands in this respect, either by a charge to the merchant or a fee collected from the customer.

In his Prairie Village center, Mr. Nichols is using a two to one parking ratio, and in Fairway, one and one-half to one where there is a high percentage of walk-in trade. In a new center he is now developing, 40 per cent of the gross site of 35 acres is being allocated to streets, 40 per cent to parking, and 20 per cent to building coverage. This is equivalent to two to one parking exclusive of streets.

(b) *Layout.* The arrangement and method of parking on any given area will, of course, affect the number of cars accommodated. In outlying centers self parking is universally used while attendant parking is customary in the central business districts. Although attendant parking will permit a greater number of cars to be parked in a given area and is generally accepted by the downtown parker, it is costly from an operational standpoint and not advisable or desirable for the community shopping center. Self parking lots require relative freedom and ease of movement. Conventional pattern is the central aisle with a tier of cars on each side. (See Figure 18.)

Head-on, right angle, or 90-degree parking has generally been found the most economical of space. The ease with which cars may be parked is an important factor, especially with women shoppers, and bears directly on the space occupied per car. Where 90 degree parking is used, a width of 65 feet has been found desirable for two tiers and a central two way aisle, although this can be reduced to 60 feet. Where 45 degree diagonal parking is used, a desirable width of 60 feet with a minimum of 55 feet is advisable. Ninety degree parking has the advantage of two way operation while other forms do not. However, the central aisle should always be wide enough to permit two cars to pass as well as to enter and leave the parking stall in one operation.

Plate XIII. A Unified Center.

HIGHLAND PARK SHOPPING VILLAGE, Dallas, Texas.

Figure 18.
Diagrams of Parking Area Layout for Shopping Centers

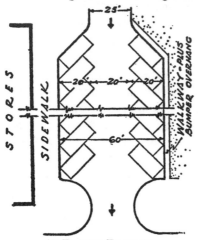

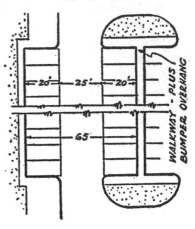

45 Degree Parking

Width of car stalls	8'-0"	9'-0"
No. of cars per 100 ft. of curb	9	8
Curb occupied per car	11'-4"	12'-9"
No. of cars per acre, excluding approaches	130	116

90 Degree—Right Angle Parking

Width of car stalls	8'-0"	9'-0"
No. of cars per 100 ft. of curb	12	11
Curb occupied per car	8'-0"	9'-0"
No. of cars per acre, excluding approaches	168	148

Note: Many developers feel the walkway between cars may be omitted.

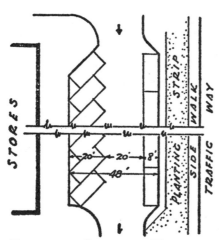

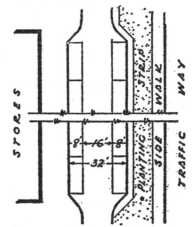

Parking in Restricted Widths

45 degree stalls—width	8'-0"	9'-0"
No. of cars per 100 ft. of curb	9	8
Parallel stalls	20'-0"	20'-0"
No. of cars per 100 ft. of curb	5	5
No. of cars per acre excluding approaches	126	117

Parking in Narrow Widths

Parallel stalls—width	20'-0"
No. of cars per 100 feet of curb	5
No. of cars per acre, excluding approaches	136

Note: Parallel parking space is seldom used as efficiently as is diagonal or right angle parking with proper marking.

Parking stalls should not be less than eight feet wide with consideration given to 8½ to 9 feet if space permits. This is particularly true for stores selling bulk cash and carry merchandise, where the ability to open car doors easily is important. Various methods of reducing the space requirements per car have been devised including the so-called herring bone pattern, different parking angles, aisle widths, and types of stall marking. These should be used only under restricted conditions and for centrally located centers, however. Local preferences and practices should be checked, especially among the women shoppers. For instance, diagonal parking appears to be preferred by women in Seattle while those in Kansas City prefer right angle parking. Foster Winter, official of The J. L. Hudson Co. of Detroit, and member of the Institute's Central Business District Council, has had field tests conducted in connection with the Detroit downtown parking program in which he is actively interested. These tests show that within a 50-foot space limitation, a double tier of cars may be parked (in 8 foot stalls) at an angle of 52½ degrees with the side line, leaving a minimum center aisle of 16 feet. The tests also show that cars can be self-parked in this manner without maneuvering into position. This arrangement is economical of space, but should be used only when space is at a premium.

Walkways between cars are favored by some developers. See Plate XV. They have the advantage of taking the shopper away from the rear of parked cars and also provide space for light standards. To be effective, however, they should lead toward the store groups. These walkways require additional space and to be usable should be approximately six feet wide to provide for walking and bumper overhang. As car doors usually open to the rear, people are in the habit of walking to the rear in parking areas. There is considerable question in the minds of some developers as to the practical use of the walkways in view of the additional cost of walks and the loss of space involved.

(c) *Loading Zones.* Off-street commercial loading zones are a feature which should be built into any center. However, where loading and unloading must be handled on streets at the curb, the developer and not the tenant should have the control over their location and in making any necessary requests of the municipal authorities. It is important to have such control over loading facilities written into all leases.

(d) *Location.* The location of parking with relation to stores is of vital importance. In old centers this feature may have to be compromised. In new projects, stores and parking should be integrated. While practice and custom vary throughout the country, the consensus is that parking areas should not be permitted to break up the continuity of store frontage. In the opinion of the Council, parking areas should not be located exclusively either to the front or rear of store groups. Rather there should be a balance between the demand during base periods, when only a portion of the parking space is occupied, and peak periods when every space will be in demand. Peak periods may represent only 15 to 20 per cent of the total number of store hours each week. Consequently, to provide all of the parking space in the front of the stores will not only set the buildings and store fronts back an excessive distance from the street, but will present a large foreground of unoccupied and unattractive paved area to the passing motorist. Conversely, if no front space is provided in the interests of window display, the motorist is discouraged in seeking a parking space, especially if rear parking is not readily discernible.

An interesting example of 100 per cent rear parking is to be found in the Westchester Business Center Development of Frank H. Ayres & Son in Los Angeles. Los Angeles was one of the first cities to experiment with the drive-in shopping center in the early twenties. Early types consisted of an L-shaped building, the front of which was usually set back a distance of 100 feet or more from the street with the entire corner in front of the stores paved for parking. This type of development enjoyed a limited success because of its novelty and its superiority to stores lacking other than curb parking space.

It soon became apparent, however, that when too many cars were parked in front of the stores, the show windows were hidden. The early type of development was then followed by the development of super-markets with wide frontage, open span structures built out to the front building line with large parking areas in the rear. This type of development drew business from the previously described centers, and was followed by various other merchants who established adjacent stores.

Plate XIV. Parking Stations Can Be Attractive!
COUNTRY CLUB PLAZA, Kansas City, Missouri.
See page 123 for description.

118

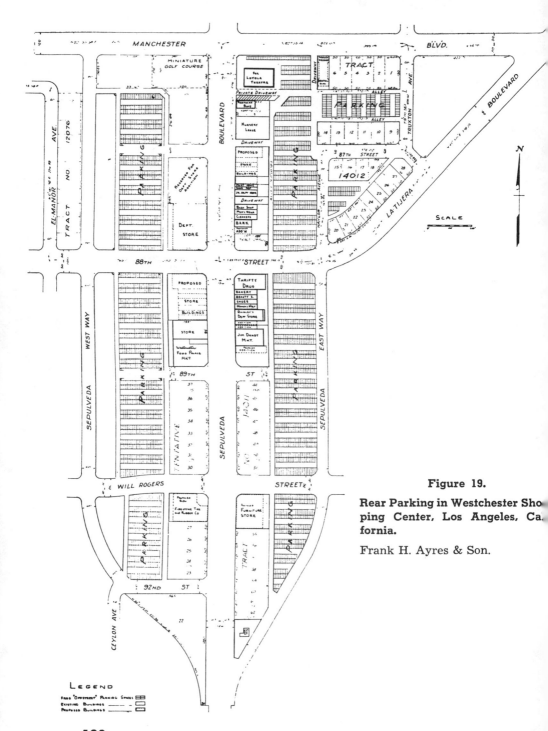

Figure 19.

Rear Parking in Westchester Shopping Center, Los Angeles, California.

Frank H. Ayres & Son.

120

Prior to establishing the Westchester Center, the Ayres Company sent out questionnaires to leading merchants together with sketches showing various parking arrangements. Opinion almost unanimously favored the main shopping area to be located along the main thoroughfare on both sides of the street, with all stores at the building line and parking in the rear to which easy access from all sides would be provided by service streets. The consensus of these replies was literally incorporated into the Westchester Center.

In commenting on the results of the questionnaire, Mr. Hayden Worthington, Manager of the Ayres Business Properties Department, says:

"In analyzing the replies which we received to our questionnaire, we found that the principal objection to front parking was the fact that the buildings necessarily had to set back too far from the street, that the show windows did not serve the purpose of calling the attention of passing traffic to the merchants' wares, that in the major business center with business on both sides of the street, it caused the stores across the street from one another to be too widely separated for free movement back and forth by shoppers, and, further, that the value of sidewalk pedestrian traffic, the most valuable and important to any volume merchant, was lost entirely by the front parking arrangement, which of necessity placed the stores back from the main street sidewalk.

"Side parking between stores was discussed. Almost all merchants considered this inadvisable for the reason that they much preferred that their show windows and store entrances immediately adjoin their neighbors rather than be separated by a parking lot and for the further reason that with side parking between merchants, of necessity, the length of the district was extended and hence pedestrians had to walk much greater distances from one merchant to another, which was judged to lessen purchases. There were a few exceptions to this, such as some grocery operators, Sears Roebuck, and other large department store developers."

This center was designed as the principal one for a minimum future population of between 40,000 and 60,000 persons. In commenting further on the Center, Mr. Worthington states:

"Our aim in the planning of Westchester was not to create the unusual, but to correct the weaknesses in shopping centers of the past that we had observed. Past faults appeared mainly to be:

"1. *Lack of parking capacity.* We have provided space for 3,500 cars in our paved off-street parking areas. Inasmuch as many of these parking spaces are used over and over again during the day, we have a capacity of serving well in excess of 10,000 cars in a day's time.

"2. *The excess of business lots in a community.* This stretched out the business areas much too far, with many unfilled spaces between buildings, marginal properties and weak marginal-type merchants. It was our purpose, therefore, to concentrate the business area into one compact center to be occupied by only top merchants and to eliminate secondary locations with cheap rents to house unsound competition.

"In placing big volume merchants in our district, we have sought to space them apart in spite of their desire to huddle close together. In this manner we are distributing the parking more evenly in the parking areas for the reason that in the end, convenience of the parking to the patron is the key to the success of the merchant. A by-product of this plan is also to enhance the opportunity for the volume of business by the smaller merchants who will be interspersed between the so-called giants.

"In the instance where we have completed a lease for the branch of a major downtown department store to occupy a building 300 feet wide by 325 feet deep, we are providing parking on the roof of this building (which will be one story in height) so as thus to not reduce our available parking area by the construction of so deep a building.

"Of vital importance, we believe, are our wide sidewalks on the main street. They are 26 feet in width."

While no formula can be established which will fit all conditions, the Council recommends that front parking space be provided slightly in excess of the average base demand expected 80 to 85 per cent of the time. This will usually form a parking area between the street and the stores accommodating two tiers of cars or a distance of approximately 70 to 75 feet from the street line to the store building line. Access to the rear parking areas should be as direct and open as possible, not only to permit cars not finding space in front to be led to the rear areas, but to overcome the resistance found in some places to rear parking such as inadequate night lighting and absence of supervision. Side parking at the end of store groups is often possible and is favored by some chain food stores. In larger centers an entire block may be allocated to parking which provides the equivalent of front parking to the surrounding stores. (Examples of various methods will be found in Figures 17 to 19 and Plates VII, VIII, XIII and XV.) The block arrangement has been used in the Country Club Plaza. J. C. Nichols comments on it as follows:

"We have two such stations in the Plaza—they serve merchants in all directions impartially. Each station has opposite entrances from two streets, which is a great help. They look like parks from the outside. The automobile entrance aisle runs through the center of the station and motorists can see any vacant stall.

"All of our merchants prefer this type of station. We only wish it were not too late to create more of them. They develop a sort of town square idea and effectively tie our merchants together all around the parking stations. The merchants' signs are visible from all over the station from boundary street to boundary street. Pedestrian exits are provided on all sides."

(e) *Appearance.* Proper maintenance of parking stations is essential if they are to continue to attract customers. This involves insuring their proper care either by the developer himself or through the merchants' association. Areas should be hard-surfaced and well drained. Paving should be of material which reflects a minimum of glare and heat, is easily repaired, and is attractive in appearance. Black top has been preferred. Parking stalls should be clearly marked. Painted markings have been abandoned by some developers in favor of white painted steel or concrete raised buttons or small "turtle-backs" of a size sufficient to discourage straddling. An oval button 8 inches in diameter and 5 inches high has been found satisfactory by J. C. Nichols.

Tree planting is desirable where adequately protected in order to break up large expanses of paved surface. Screen plantings for rear parking areas should be provided, especially where there is abutting residential property. This is required in some zoning ordinances. In the Country Club District, Kansas City, the parking areas, which cover an entire block in some cases, are depressed about 2 feet in order to lower the car tops below eye level, increase the feeling of openness and permit vision across the surrounding streets.

123

(f) *Operation.* The operation of free parking stations in out-lying shopping centers is recommended by the Council. Continuation of this practice is rendered difficult in some cities where land used exclusively for parking purposes is evaluated at the same level as that used for business. In the Council's opinion, this is an inequitable and questionable practice. Many cities are now undertaking the provision of municipal tax free parking lots where parking fees are collected and which will contribute substantially to relieving streets of the congestion of traffic and parked cars. Where commitments are made for the continued use of designated areas for parking, it is believed that the tax valuation should be adjusted to the restricted use to which the land is put. While it is true that off-street parking facilities contribute substantially to the success of any given business in the center, it is equally true that this is reflected in the higher taxable value of land and structure containing the business as well as the business itself. As the parking area of itself is usually neither an existing nor potential revenue producer, its valuation for tax purposes should be adjusted accordingly. Some municipalities follow this practice with good results. Valuation of large areas as acreage rather than on a square foot basis is suggested.

Items of policing, clean-up, night lighting, and orderly use, should not be ignored. Some members of the Council have permitted a car washing, shoe shine stand, or other similar service, to be operated by one or more persons who in return police and clean the lot. In some cases the merchants' association maintains the stations. David Bohannon is providing a central control tower in his Hillsdale project in order to spot vacant parking stalls and direct traffic to them during rush hours.

5. Store Types.

Experience has shown that normally it requires a minimum of about 500 families to support a small shopping center. With this nucleus a maximum of about 10 stores can be considered. The Council members, after detailed consideration based on many years of experience in the development and operation of centers of various sizes and types, have developed a list of 30

Plate XV. A Carefully Studied Project.
"HILLSDALE" SHOPPING CENTER,
San Mateo, California.

124

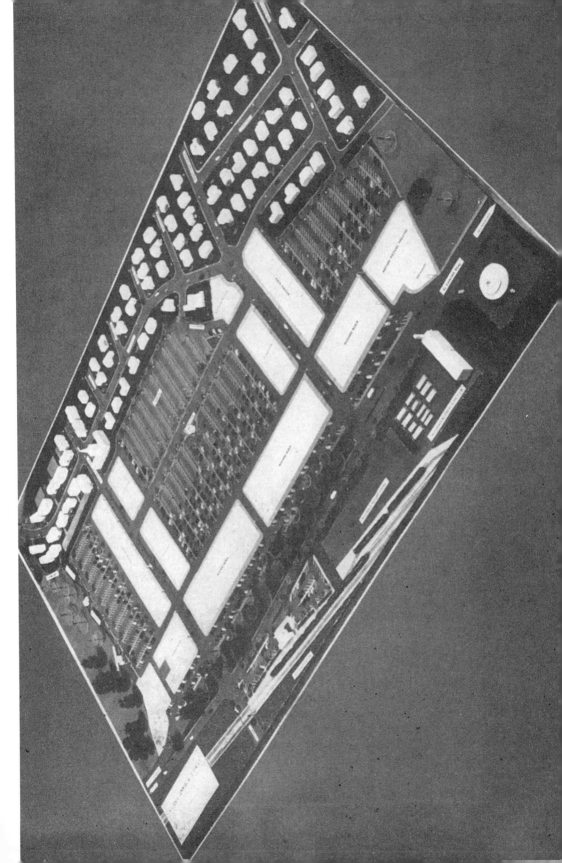

Plate XVI. Section of Shopping Center.
San Lorenzo Village, California. David D. Bohannon Organization.

store types arranged in the general order in which they should be established in the center. If the developer is fortunate enough to obtain a major store with high drawing power as the initial unit in his center, this should be done. This situation is the exception, however, and under normal conditions the center would be built up around the recommendations below, subject, of course, to variation in different localities with local habits and customs, amount of walk-in trade, and size of the tributary area.

1. Drug Store (with some eating facilities)

2. Cash and Carry Grocery

3. Cleaner and Dyer shop which could be combined with a laundry agency *

4. Beauty Parlor *

5. Filling Station *

6. Bakery (this might depend on bakery provided by supermarket)

 7. Shoe Repair—possibly in rear of another store or combined with cleaner and dyer

8. Laundry Agency—possibly in rear of another shop or combined with cleaner and dyer *

9. Variety Store—possibly on a temporary basis

10. Barber Shop *

The next ten businesses which would be added as the center develops are in order of importance.

11. Service Grocery with phone order and delivery service

12. Florist

13. Milliner

14. Radio and Electrical Shop *

15. Five and Ten Cent Store

16. Shoes—children and repairs

17. Gift Shop

18. Candy and Nut Shop

19. Lingerie and Hosiery

20. Liquor Store *

---

* These shops could be moved from the 100% location as the center develops.

Further development of the center would call for the following additional stores in order of importance.

21. "Fix It" Shop—a small shop repairing locks, key fitting, lawn mower sharpening and similar services *
22. Dress Shop—popular prices with children's wear
23. Theatre—be sure of ample drawing power
24. Frozen Foods—possibly with rental food lockers *
25. Cafe or Drive-In Restaurant *
26. Book and Stationery Shop
27. Dentists and Physicians—possibly second floor location
28. Baby and Toy Shop
29. Haberdashery—not including clothing
30. Athletic Goods *

These should be considered as the 30 most important neighborhood stores.

Further development of a shopping center will probably necessitate shifts in location of certain stores from "front" to side locations, the increase in floor area of some which have outgrown their original space requirements, and possibly the decrease in others. Many a merchant has failed or never makes progress because of the initial burden of too large a space and too much overhead. Ability to fit space to the changing needs of the tenant cannot be overemphasized. It should be emphasized also that the developer in selecting stores for his center must consider the service it is to render to the neighborhood as well as to the amount of revenue to be derived. All types of stores cannot and should not pay the same rental per square foot. The tenant should be made aware of the fact that his rent is to be based upon the probable volume and profit of his particular type of business. Certain types of businesses such as banks, post offices, and other service establishments, usually pay low rentals and may even lose money for the developer. They are, however, extremely valuable to high rent tenants in drawing power, and round-out the service to the community which is essential in maintaining continued patronage and good will. It is also important that the developer control by lease the type of merchandise which any one tenant will sell. While reasonable competi-

---

* These shops could be moved from the 100% location as the center develops.

tion is desirable, the established tenant should be protected against undue competition from newcomers or the introduction of competitive lines by other existing tenants. This protection of the tenant is a valuable consideration which should properly be reflected in the rent he has to pay, and, of course, this is a constantly changing picture in a growing center.

6. Store Grouping.

Grouping of stores within the center with relation to their merchandise and type of service is an extremely important factor in the success of a shopping center, especially a large one. Certain stores complement each other and should be located together, while others tend to injure adjacent stores. For instance, shops catering to women should be close together; service, grocery, and five-and-ten-cent stores complement each other; garages, filling stations, and auto sales rooms should be closely related; service and repair shops should be grouped; and such types as hardware, electrical repair, and furniture are supplementary. In the large center, such complementary groups should in turn be located with reference to so-called "hot spot" or 100 per cent location which may be a particular corner or may include a block or more within the center. The factors which should determine the distribution of these groups are: (1) amount of rent, (2) convenience to the community, and (3) suitability of the shop for the location. There should be less attention given to the amount of return derived from any one shop than to the objective of obtaining and holding the community trade and maintaining the center as a whole in a prosperous condition.

Many surveys have been made of the types and existing groupings of stores in our urban areas. This information has been of great value in studying the nature of and area needed for business development. However, the Council feels these studies to be entirely inadequate because they are merely a measure of existing conditions which, if followed blindly, would simply repeat past mistakes. Rarely has consideration been given to the effect of proper interrelated store grouping on the prosperity of the business area as a whole, which in turn is directly reflected in increased income. The Council has given long and intensive study to this matter and feels that the results which appear on the following pages are unique and of especial value, not only to the shopping center developer, but to the downtown merchant and property owner as well.

With the above factors in mind the Council has studied 308 types of business establishments and grouped them alphabetically into 4 lists on the basis of location. Those in Number 1 are recommended for location in or adjacent to the 100 per cent or "hot spot", while Number 2, 3 and 4 types include establishments which should normally be in side locations progressively farther away from the center's hot spot. There are, of course, a number of borderline cases as well as cases where a second floor location is preferable if available. A case in point is the beauty parlor which, if on the first floor, occupies valuable retail frontage. It is important, however, to avoid preferential treatment where there are two or more stores of the same type in the center. If two beauty parlors are located in the center, both should be in second floor locations if such space is available.

Office buildings or office space to accommodate any sizable office organizations are not included in the list. They are not desirable as a rule in outlying centers, increase trade very little, and unless rigidly controlled, will usurp all day parking space which should be reserved for shoppers. If a developer intends to sell any land in the center, it should be done only after placing restrictions on it as to future use, enforceable by the developer, which will be in line with his overall development plan for the center. Professional offices, particularly doctors and dentists where they occur in any number, are in the same category. They are expensive tenants, janitor service alone running about twice that of other tenants. Where they cannot be accommodated in second floor locations, the provision of a semi-residential type of building located to act as a buffer between the center and adjacent residential development is a satisfactory solution.

Large mail order stores, while creating drawing power, usually pay a low rental and require one use buildings which are expensive. They may also make it difficult for certain local shops, such as hardware, to compete successfully. Branch department stores, as a rule, are less aggressive than an individual store and generally pay much lower rentals. However, this type of store is favored by some developers to form the nucleus around which to develop a center. Municipal buildings, including fire and

Plate XVII. **Modern Store Fronts Increase Display Area.**
FARRINGTON BUILDING, Village Shopping Center, Houston, Texas. William G. Farrington Co.

police stations, have a definite deadening effect on adjoining retail frontage and should be placed in side locations if at all possible.

The list below should be considered as a reference and check list. It represents the considered opinion of the Council which recognizes that specific local conditions may dictate the relocation of certain store types. It is recommended, however, that such relocations be made only after a thorough analysis of the particular case.

No. 1 Locations.
(100 Per Cent or "Hot Spot")

1. Bakery.
2. Bookstore.
3. Boys' Clothing.
4. Candy Store.
5. Children's wear.
6. Cosmetics and Perfume.
7. Costume Jewelry.
8. Department Store. (Trend is toward branches of downtown stores.)
9. Drug Store.
10. Five & Ten Cent Store. (Trend of chains is toward outlying centers.)
11. Florist.
12. Fruit Juices.
13. Furs. (No. 2 if storage included.)
14. Gift Shop.
15. Girls' Apparel Shop.
16. Grocery Store—Cash and Carry.
17. Handkerchiefs and Handbags.
18. Hosiery Shop.
19. Infants' Wear and Baby Shop.
20. Jewelry and Diamond Store.
21. Lingerie.
22. Leather Goods. (Depends on ability to pay high rent.)
23. Luggage. (Depends on ability to pay high rent.)
24. Men's Furnishings.
25. Men's Clothing Store.
26. Millinery.
27. Novelty Store.
28. Parking Stations. (Customers Only.)

All leases should prohibit employers or employees from parking their cars in the No. 1 parking stations. These parking stations should normally be held at the edge of the 100 per cent district, if possible, so as not to break the continuity of shops. Employees' parking should be in the second, third, or, if possible, fourth locations even if a walk of two or three blocks is required.

29. Photographic Supplies, Cameras, etc. (Rent is a factor.)
30. Pop Corn and Nut Shop.
31. Prescription Shop. (Separate prescription shops may have an adverse effect on the drugstore)
32. Restaurant. (In most cities restaurants are going to outlying centers.)
33. Shoes, Women's.
34. Shoes, Men's.
35. Shoes, Children's.
36. Soft Drinks.
37. Sportswear—Women's.
38. Tobacco Shop.
39. Toilet Goods.
40. Variety Store.
41. Women's Wearing Apparel.

The following shops may go equally well in either No. 1 or No. 2 locations:

1. Cafeteria. (In all cities there is a great increase of cafeterias in neighborhood centers.)
2. Dry Goods Store.
3. Grocery Store. (Service)
4. News Store.

No. 1 Locations should be held largely for shops which will keep open on certain common nights.

No. 2 Locations.
(Near 100 Per Cent Area)

1. Art Shop and Artists' Supplies.
2. Athletic Goods Store.
3. Automobile Supplies.
4. Bank.

A bank has good pulling power, but it should not be in a No. 1 location as it has limited "open" hours and when closed has a deadening effect on adjacent shops.

New outlying banks often provide a window where deposits can be made by automobile.

There is a trend in many cities for banks to go to outlying centers.

5. Bar (liquor).
6. Barber Shop. (Basement in the No. 1 location)

When deciding on width of barber shop, consider carefully the number of lines of barber chairs in order that space will not be wasted.

134

7. Beauty Shop. (No. 2 Location or second floor in No. 1.)
8. Butcher Shop.
9. China and Silver Shop.
10. Cleaners and Dyers (Pick-up). (This can go to No. 3 in some cases.)
11. Cocktail Lounge. (In all cities many are in outlying centers.)
12. Corset Shop. (This may go in No. 3 in some cases, or 2nd floor in No. 1.)
13. Delicatessen. (Also No. 1 in some cases.)
14. Electrical Appliances. (Also No. 3.)
15. Filling Stations. (Also No. 3 and No. 4.)

Filling station leases should be made on vacant land. If the land becomes too valuable, they can ultimately be moved.

16. Frozen Food Mart. (Also No. 3 or 4.)
17. Fruit and Vegetable Market. (Should be considered in relation to regular grocers.)
18. Glass and China.
19. Laundry Agency.
20. Linen Shop. (Possibly No. 1.)
21. Liquor Store.
22. Maternity Clothes Shop.
23. Pen shop. (Also No. 1— as they are high rent payers.)
24. Parking Stations.

These parking stations should serve strictly the overflow of customers from No. 1 Locations and No. 2 customers, and if space is ample, for employers and employees from No. 1 and No. 2 Locations. It is better if employers' and employees' parking stations are removed as far as No. 3 or 4, if possible.

25. Radio Shop.
26. Sewing Machine Shop and Supplies.
27. Sporting Goods.
28. Stationery and Greeting Cards. (Can sometimes be located in No. 1.)
29. Telegraph Office.
30. Theater. (Or No. 3.)
31. Woolen Shop.

If theater crowds are large, and if matinees are held, parking stations may be filled by theater crowds during store hours. The customers form a line in front of other merchants' front doors. Restaurants like to be close to theaters. In all cities many theaters are moving to outlying centers.

The following shops may go equally well in either No. 2 or No. 3 locations:

1. Gas, and power and light company offices. Many people pay bills personally. They need parking.
2. Shoe Shining. (Or in other shops.)
3. Toy Shop.

No. 3 Locations.

1. Army Goods Store. (Also No. 4.)
2. Art Needlework Shop.
3. Baby Furniture.
4. Baby Foods.
5. Building & Loan Office.
6. Button Hole Shop. (Also second floor in No. 1 or No. 2.)
7. Cab Stand.
8. Chinese Restaurant.
9. Christian Science Reading Room. (Or 2nd floor in No. 2.)
10. Dance Studio. (Or No. 4.)
11. Doctors and Dentists. (Or second floor in No. 2.)

Some developers do not favor doctors and dentists in central areas of outlying shopping centers.

The janitor expense for doctors' and dentists' offices is at least twice as high as for ordinary office space. Also, they are the hardest tenants to please as to maintenance.

12. Drapery & Curtain Store.
13. Electric Repair Shop.
14. Electric Equipment (large items).
15. Express Office. (Popular service.)
    Express office will help you build up a district.
16. Fix-it Shop.
17. Furniture Shop. (Pay low rent per square foot.)
18. Hardware.
19. Health Foods Store.
20. Hobby Shop.
21. Interior Decoration. (Also No. 2.)
22. Knit Shop.
23. Ladies' Tailor. (Or second floor in No. 1 or No. 2.)
24. Lending Library. (Or No. 4.)
25. Men's Tailor. (Or second floor in No. 1 or No. 2.)
26. Mortgage Loan Office. (Or second floor in No. 2.)
27. Office Supplies and Office Furniture. (Or No. 4. Pay low rent per square foot.)
28. Optometrist and Oculist. (Or second floor No. 1 or No. 2.)
29. Poultry Shop, Sales Only. (Popular in some cities.)
30. Parking Stations.

These stations should provide for customers and employees of No. 3 Location and all-day parking for employers and employees from No. 1 Location and possibly No. 2 Location. If parking fees are charged on any of the stations, all-day parking should be at very low rates in No. 3 and No. 4 Locations.

31. Paint Store.
32. Photographers. (Or second floor in No. 1 or No. 2.)
33. Piano Store. (Low rent.)
34. Picture Frames. (Low rent.)
35. Post Office. (Or No. 2.)

An important center should have a post office and it requires adequate parking space.

Post offices in connection with super-markets have proved successful in Los Angeles.

36. Power and Light Offices. (This brings a lot of people to pay bills—adequate parking needed.) (Or No. 2.)
37. Railroad Ticket Office. (Or No. 2.)
38. Real Estate Office. (Or No. 4.)
39. Savings & Loan Association. (Or No. 4.)
40. Shoe Repair Shop.
41. Tavern. (Adequate parking is required.)
42. Telephone Company Office. (Or No. 4.)
43. Transient Hotel. (Or No. 4.)
44. Travel Bureau, Separate. (Or No. 2.)

A Travel Bureau in connection with a luggage shop will bring customers.

45. Vitamin Shop. (Should be combined with drug store.)
46. Watch Repairs. (Should be in jewelry shop.)

The following shops may go equally well in No. 3 and No. 4 Locations:

1. Bus Terminal. Bus terminals build up rentals; however, people may leave their cars parked at the terminal all day.
2. Night Club. Popular. (Needs parking.)
3. Library. Branch libraries are increasing.

No. 4 Locations
(FARTHEST FROM 100 PER CENT LOCATION)

1. Art Studios. (Or second floor in No. 2 or 3.)
2. Architects. (Or second floor.)
3. Auditors. (Or second floor.)
4. Airplane Sales Lots. Low rent.
5. Addressograph Shop.
6. Air Conditioning Distributors.
7. Air Conditioning Shop, sales. (Many such shops are being established.)
8. Athletic Club.
9. Automatic Family Laundry Service. (Popular in some cities.)
10. Automobile Agencies, sales only. (Require large space.)
11. Awnings — sale and display room.
12. Battery Shop. (Or in auto service shops).
13. Bowling Alleys.

Bowling alleys are going to outlying shopping areas. They do a big night business and a cocktail lounge and cafe do well in connection with them. They will bring a lot of trade to other merchants. They should have adequate parking.

14. Bath and Massage. (Or second floor, or basement.)
15. Bathroom Fixtures and Plumbing Supplies. Low rent.
16. Bicycle Shop. Popular in some cities.
17. Blue Print Shop.
18. Building Contractor's Office.
19. Building Materials, sales. Low rent but essential.
20. Business Schools. Need a lot of parking. (Many are decentralizing).
21. Barbecue. (Also No. 3 Location).
22. Carbonated Water Firms, sales.
23. Carpenter Shop. Very essential.
24. Carpets and Rugs, Cleaning. Very popular.
25. Chicken Dinner Eating Places. Need a lot of parking.
26. Chick Hatchery.
27. Churches.

Churches should not be in the business center. They make a good buffer and should have ample off-street parking.

28. Club House. (Men and women). Need parking.
29. Coal and fuel sales office.
30. Commercial Offices. (Or second floor). (Many are decentralizing).
31. Contractors' Offices. Essential.
32. Correspondence Schools.
33. Creameries, sales. Very popular.
34. Chiropodist. (Or second floor in No. 2 or 3).
35. Chiropractor. (Or second floor in No. 2 or 3).
36. Costumes, rental.
37. Dairy Agencies. Popular.
38. Dog and Cat Hospital. Quite popular and essential.
39. Dramatic School. Needs parking.
40. Drive-it-yourself place.
41. Dance Hall. Popular. (Needs parking).

Some developers have eliminated dance halls because of policing difficulty and the large demand for parking.

42. Dressmakers. (Or second floor in No. 2 or No. 3).
43. Drive-in Eating Places. Popular. Need parking.
44. Drive-in Ice Cream, sales.
45. Dental Laboratories. (Or second floor—should be near dentists' offices).
46. Diaper Service.
47. Electricians.
48. Employment Agency. (Or second floor).
49. Engineers' Offices. (Or second floor).
50. Electric Light Fixtures. Pay low rent per square foot.
51. Embroidery. (Or second floor No. 2 or No. 3).
52. Fire and Police Department.
53. Funeral Home. Needs ample off-street parking.
54. Furnace Sales and Repair.
55. Fur Storage and Fur Repair.
56. Furniture Repair. Essential.
57. Filling Stations. (Or in other locations except No. 1).

Filling stations are good paying investments. Cost of free parking can be reduced by using a corner of a parking station for a service station.

58. Fish bait, tackle, etc.
59. Furniture, second-hand. Essential.
60. Garage and minor repairs, etc.
61. Gunsmith.

62. Greenhouses. Can be a buffer.

63. Gymnasium and Sports Center. Needs parking.

64. Hamburger Stand. (Also No. 2 or No. 3).

65. Hemstitching Shop. (Or second floor in No. 2 or No. 3).

66. House Equipment Display Rooms. Pay low rent.

67. Health Club. (Or second floor).

68. Heating Contractor.

69. House cleaning and repair. Essential.

70. House Movers.

71. Hospital Supplies.

72. Hospital. Needs a large amount of off-street parking. Can be a buffer. Trend is to outlying sites.

73. Ice Cream (package) and Milk (bottled). Can pay high rental. Popular.

74. Insulating Shop, sales. Popular.

75. Insurance Agency. (Or second floor in No. 2 or 3).

76. Investment and Security Office.

77. Kindergartens. Need parking.

78. Key and Lock Service. (Or in hardware stores or fix-it shops).

79. Landscape Office. (Or second floor in No. 3).

80. Landscape Achitect. (Or second floor in No. 3).

81. Lawn sprinklers, sales.

82. Lawn and soil service. Can be at the edge of the center. Popular.

83. Lodges (Mason, Eastern Star, etc.). Need a lot of off-street parking. Many are moving to outlying residential areas.

84. Lumber yard, building materials and supplies. Essential. Should be placed to not injure neighborhood if permitted.

85. Letter Service Shop. (Or second floor in No. 2 or No. 3).

86. Linoleum. (Or in furniture or carpet store).

87. Manufacturers' agents. (Or second floor in No. 2 or 3).

88. Mattress Shop, sales. (Or in furniture store).

89. Miniature Golf. Popular in some cities. This is a good temporary use for vacant land. Should be on a short term lease. They need off-street parking.

90. Motorboats.

91. Monument Company.

92. Music Schools. (Or second floor). Many are moving to residential areas.

93. Nurses' Registry. (Or second floor). Perhaps could be combined with "sitters" agency.

94. Nursery, sales — t r e e s, plants, seeds, etc. Popular. This is a good temporary use of vacant land. They can go to the edge of the district.
95. Oil Burner Shop. Essential.
96. Ornamental Iron (sales or repair).
97. Osteopath. (Or second floor in No. 2 or No. 3).
98. Plumbers. Very essential. Can often go in a basement if there is good ramp access.
99. Paper Hangers. Essential.
100. Parking stations (for employees of all groups).

Parking stations here should provide for customers and employees in No. 4 Locations and the overflow of employers' and employees' all-day cars from No. 1, 2 and 3.

101. Plastics. Increasing in popularity and may go to No. 2 or No. 3.
102. Pool and Billiard Place. These are coming more and more into suburban centers. Need a lot of parking.

103. Painters.
104. Pest exterminating. (Or second floor.)
105. Pony ring. Good temporary use.
106. P r i n t i n g shop, small hand press. Essenti:l.
107. Private schools. Need parking. (Good buffers.)
108. Quilting Shop. (Or second floor in No. 2 or No. 3.)
109. Radio Station. Many going to outlying areas.
110. Recreation Center. Needs parking. (Good buffer.)
111. Research laboratories. (Or second floor.)
112. Roofing place, sales.
113. Sanitariums. Many are decentralizing.
114. Screens and repairs. Essential.
115. Secretarial schools. (Or second floor.) Need parking.
116. Sheet metal.
117. Sign shop, sales or small signs.
118. Sign painters. (In rear of some shops.)
119. Storage and transfer.
120. Sypho, carbonated water shop, sales.
121. Skating rink. (Roller rinks noisy.)
122. Swimming Pool. Needs lots of parking. Difficult to police—noisy.
123. Television Equipment. Put with radio shop.
124. Taxidermist. (Or second floor.)
125. Television and F.M. stations.
126. Termite control. (Or second floor.) Essential.

127. Towel service. (Or second floor.) Essential.
128. Tourist court. (At edge of district.) Many go farther out.
129. Trailer sales place. Temporary use. Popular.
130. Tree expert service. (Or second floor.)
131. Tires.
132. Typewriter and Adding Machine Repairs. (Or in a basement.)
133. Upholstering shop. (Or with furniture store.) Essential.
134. Used car lot. Temporary use. Can be objectionable to neighborhood.

135. Uniform Shop. (Or in No. 3.)
136. Ventilating equipment.
137. Veterinarian. (Or second floor.)
138. Washing machine repair shop. Can go in basement.
139. Weatherstrip shop. Can go in basement.
140. Wholesale electrical.
141. Wholesale florist offices. Many are decentralizing.
142. Wholesale plumbing. Many are decentralizing.
143. Window washing. Can go in basement. Essential.

Miscellaneous.

144. X-Ray Laboratories. (Or second floor in No. 2 or 3.) Best with medical group.

145. Small Emergency Hospital. Desirable near medical group in No. 2 or 3.

The following establishments should be on the second floor only:

1. Advertising Agency.
2. Artists' Studio.
3. Lawyers.
4. Notary Public.
5. Public Accountants.
6. Stenographers' Office (Public)

The factors taken into consideration in determining the location of the above shops were: (1) amount of rent, (2) convenience to the community, (3) suitability of shop for location, (4) trade pulling power, and (5) parking needs.

When center is small, there will be certain merchants and service shops in the No. 1 Location, which as the center grows should be moved to another location—in No. 2 or No. 3, or even No. 4.

7. Suggested Layouts of Progressive Types of Shopping Centers.

Small neighborhoods of scattered houses usually are dependent on distant centers for shopping facilities, except where there are small independent owner-operated stores carrying limited amounts of food and other frequently used commodities.

A more concentrated community of one hundred families would best be served by a single store or market building dispensing the usual frequent or daily family purchases. Such a structure would approximate 2500 sq. ft. of floor space.

When 250 or more families constitute a well defined community and there are practically no stores within a radius of one-half mile, a minor shopping center installation may be practical.

The two plans below are typical of the many varied arrangements of the stores usually to be found in this size group. The breaks shown in store fronts are not recommended.

For the minor store group serving neighborhoods of approximately 250 to 300 families, there is an infinite variety of arrangements. (a) and (b) in Figure 20 show types of this character.

Figure 20.

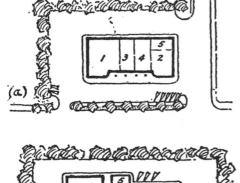

1. Food Supplies		3,500 sq. ft.
2. Drugs and	Variety	2,000 sq. ft.
3. Beauty Parlor and	Barber Shop	800 sq. ft.
4. Cleaning, Laundry	Agency	300 sq. ft.
5. Service, Heating,	etc.	300 sq. ft.
		6,900 sq. ft.

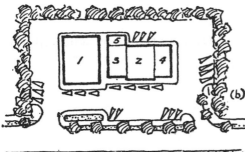

APPROXIMATE STORE AREAS

1. Food Supplies		3,600 sq. ft.
2. Drug and	Variety	3,000 sq. ft.
3. Beauty Parlor and Barber	Shop	850 sq. ft.
4. Cleaning, Laundry and Shoe	Repair	750 sq. ft.
5. Service, Heating, etc.		400 sq. ft.
		8,600 sq. ft.

143

Figure 21.

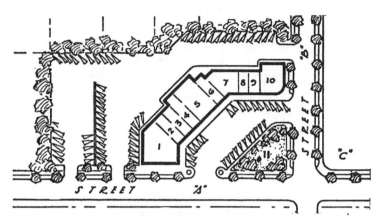

A shopping center of this type is practical when the two streets A and B are of nearly equal importance or when A is the main highway and B is the principal entrance to an extensive neighborhood. Should the corner C be built up to obscure the approach view of stores 8, 9 and 10, then this plan is less desirable.

From the point of view of the market location the large adjacent parking lot is a valued asset.

1. Market	3,800 sq. ft.
2. Cleaner & Dyer	700 "
3. Ladies Wear	900 "
4. Beauty Shop	700 "
5. Variety	1,950 "
6. Bakery	600 "
7. Delicatessen and lunch	1,200 "
8. Shoe Repair & Laundry	600 "
9. Barber	600 "
10. Drugs	2,400 "
	13,450 "
11. Gas Station	— "

Many members of the Council question the practicability of this layout because it lacks pedestrian pulling power.

Figure 22.
A Practical Shopping Center to Serve 500 to 600 Families

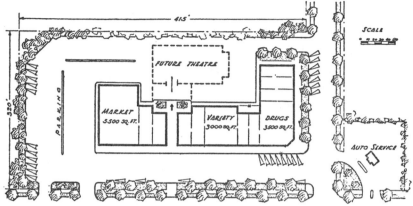

Might support a small theater and gas station.

Figure 23.
A Shopping Center For 500 to 700 Families

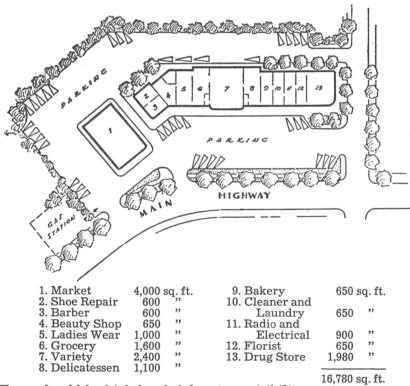

1. Market	4,000 sq. ft.		9. Bakery	650 sq. ft.
2. Shoe Repair	600 "		10. Cleaner and	
3. Barber	600 "		Laundry	650 "
4. Beauty Shop	650 "		11. Radio and	
5. Ladies Wear	1,000 "		Electrical	900 "
6. Grocery	1,600 "		12. Florist	650 "
7. Variety	2,400 "		13. Drug Store	1,980 "
8. Delicatessen	1,100 "			16,780 sq. ft.

Trees should be high headed for store visibility.

The outstanding features of the plan in Figure 23 are as follows:

(1) Preferential location of the three principal stores, Market (1), Variety (7), and Drug Store (13).

(2) Ample parking in front with over-flow in rear.

(3) Market is independent of other stores with its own parking space.

(4) Middle section (stores 6, 7, and 8) can be two stories in height to accommodate offices above.

(5) Easy access to secondary street from both front and rear parking.

(6) Variation in widths and depth of stores.

(7) Trees planted at side and in rear of stores help to screen buildings from the residential section.

Figure 24.

Modern Type of Shopping Center for a Small Community of 500 to 700 Families

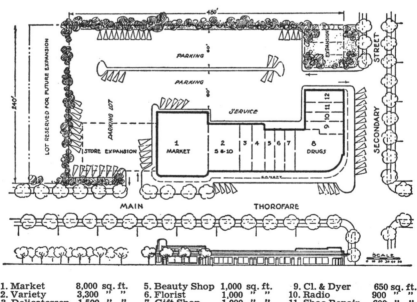

1. Market	8,000 sq. ft.	5. Beauty Shop	1,000 sq. ft.	9. Cl. & Dyer	650 sq. ft.
2. Variety	3,300 " "	6. Florist	1,000 " "	10. Radio	900 " "
3. Delicatessen	1,500 " "	7. Gift Shop	1,000 " "	11. Shoe Repair	600 " "
4. Ladies Wear	1,500 " "	8. Drugs	3,200 " "	12. Hardware	2,000 " "

This small shopping center illustrates many of the principles approved by the Community Builders' Council. However, it must be emphasized that there is no model or ideal shopping center plan, as custom, shopping habits, and local conditions vary widely in every city and for every separate site. In actual practice breaks in the store fronts should be avoided.

Figure 25.

Plan of Shopping Center to Serve 750 to 1000 Families

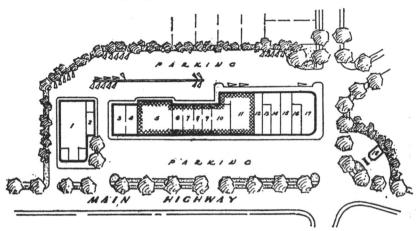

The above plan is drawn to show two stages of construction. The shaded portion, being the initial installation, comprises seven stores with the Market (5), and Drug Store (11), flanking the two ends. The remaining stores and theater could be erected progressively as required, with necessary shifts of store location.

1. Theater	7,500 sq. ft.	11. Drug Store	5,000 sq. ft.
2. Barber	1,000 " "	12. Shoes	1,350 " "
3. Radio & Electrical	1,800 " "	13. Cleaner & Laundry	900 " "
4. Liquor	1,440 " "	14. Bakery	2,000 " "
5. Super Market	7,500 " "	15. Independent Grocer	1,500 " "
6. Gift Shop	1,300 " "	16. Books & Stationery	900 " "
7. Beauty Parlor	1,300 " "	17. Restaurant	3,000 " "
8. Ladies Wear	1,300 " "	18. Gas Station	10,000 " "
9. Haberdashery	1,300 " "		
10. Variety (5 & 10c)	2,600 " "		51,690 sq. ft.

Population   3,500
Area of Stores   51,690 sq. ft.
Frontage of Stores, 550 lin. ft.   15.7 per 100 people
Store Area   0.34 acre per 1,000 people

In actual practice these floor areas may vary widely from those shown, depending on the local situation.

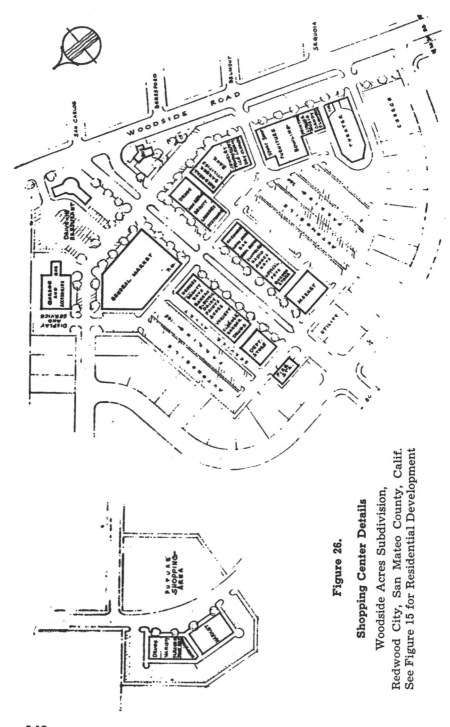

Figure 26.

Shopping Center Details

Woodside Acres Subdivision,
Redwood City, San Mateo County, Calif.
See Figure 15 for Residential Development

C. ARCHITECTURAL AND STRUCTURAL DESIGN OF SHOPPING CENTERS.

1. External Appearance.

While the basic organization relating to store grouping, building, and parking space arrangement is fundamental in the design of shopping centers, it is also important that this organization be reflected in the architectural appearance of the buildings. A considerable degree of unity in the type of building design is recommended. Many of the older successful centers went in for architectural styles including distinctive details such as towers, balconies, and other ornamental features. While these additional features have proved to be well worth their cost, the trend toward simple design along modern lines has the advantage of less cost and greater flexibility for present use and future adaptation to changing conditions. Greater reliance is put on proportion and form rather than on embellishment. Extreme "modernistic" designs should be avoided, however, as they may be quickly outdated and less acceptable than good period styles such as Colonial, Mission, English, Spanish, etc. The developer should retain control over the approval of exterior design, even though he sells one or more parts of the center.

(a) *Show Windows.* Good modern shopping center design calls for the maximum of glass front on the first floor with low bulkheads, especially where large items are to be displayed. Mullioned or divided windows should be avoided. Bulkheads as low as 6 to 8 inches have been found desirable for some types of merchandise. This type of front gives a maximum of flexibility as it permits maximum window displays, but is equally adaptable to "spot light" displays for small items, such as jewelry, by painting out or draping the unused glass area with the minimum of interior alteration. This avoids the excessive costs of bulkhead removal, new glass, etc., involved in heavy masonry construction and will save the developer unnecessary expense in the future. Exterior bulkheads of granite veneer require less maintenance than other materials. Aluminum or stainless steel window trim is recommended instead of brass and copper for the same reason.

(b) *Canopies.* Canopies are becoming increasingly popular, especially in sections of the country with a high rainfall and summer heat, although snow removal may be a problem in some sections of the country. The canopy can be made an attractive architectural feature. The type developed at River Oaks by Hugh Potter is worth noting. The under surface curves upward from the show window to a height of 13 feet above the sidewalk at the outer edge. Width is 7 feet. Top provides enough slope for rainwater drainage toward the building. A space just above the show windows is reserved for signs. Horizontal and tilted canopies have also been used successfully and have proved to be well worth the additional cost. Drop awnings may be necessary in addition to protect merchandise from the sun, although this will depend on orientation and latitude. Research is being conducted on a new type of glass which will protect displays from direct sunlight.

(c) *Off-sets*. Although many architects will recommend off-sets in store fronts for architectural effect, it has been found to be undesirable as the recessed store is partly hidden from view. Off-sets of only a few feet, or even a few inches, have been found to affect store values and rentals adversely. This applies equally to the so-called court group where the inside corner store space is less valuable.

The location of store entrances is a very important item which should not be left to the decision of the architect. This is illustrated by a hardware store which occupied a corner location. The original entrance was moved from a side to a front location, a distance of less than 25 feet, resulting in doubling the merchant's business in the first six months.

Avoid all entrance steps and ramps. They are definite deterrents to business as well as hazards to pedestrians.

(d) *Signs*. One of the things which disgraces the business districts of American cities both central and outlying, along with poor architecture, is the indiscriminate use of signs. This is particularly true of the colored illuminated sign. In many centers the original purpose of directing attention to a particular shop has been lost in the effort of shops to outdo each other. The result is chaotic, confusing, and self-defeating. The Council favors strongly a reasonable control over signs in shopping centers, both as to size, design, location, and color of illumination. As examples, J. C. Nichols is limiting all future signs in his shopping centers to a maximum of 8 to 12-inch letters. Where illuminated, white lighting only will be permitted, and in the smaller centers signs will be unilluminated. Waverly Taylor limits signs to a belt course above the canopy to an overall height of 2 feet and a length of 2/3 of the shop front. Hugh Potter restricts signs to an area under the canopy and directly above the show window. Overhanging, roof, and projecting signs should be prohibited as should the use of paper signs attached to the show windows. Elimination of such signs will enhance the character and attractiveness of the center. Experience with such controls has shown that they are appreciated by the public and are eventually supported by the merchants who operate within the center although often opposed in the beginning.

Regarding the problem of signs, the Council adopted the following resolution: *WHEREAS the indiscriminate use of signs and billboards in suburban commercial areas, and particularly on the main approaches to our cities, is ugly, unsightly, and objectionable; creates an unfavorable opinion of the city in the minds of visitors; and is injurious to all urban property values: Therefore, be it RESOLVED that developers of suburban shopping centers be urged to exercise reasonable and proper controls of all signs placed on properties which they control.*

2. Basements.

Experience has shown that the omission of basements has usually been a mistake. They have proved their value not only for storage, heating, and cooling equipment, but even to a greater extent, as space for store expansion. The additional cost of providing basement space is relatively low, especially in sections of the country requiring foundation footings 3 to 4 feet below grade. It has been found in many cases that basements are superior to mezzanines for merchandising and store offices. Thus the extra store height necessary for mezzanines can be eliminated. This has the further advantage where a second floor is provided of making it more easily accessible to the public. It is advisable in providing basements to anticipate their future use as merchandising space. Pipes and ducts should be located with this in mind and clear ceiling heights of about 9 feet should be provided for all but small shops where 8 feet could be used satisfactorily.

Cost saving features in basement construction include the use of concrete block foundations where subsurface conditions permit, and supporting the first floor on transverse beams. This eliminates the need for basement stair headers and permits future basement stairs to be relocated and widened without undue expense. This is an important contribution in providing the maximum amount of flexibility in revising store space and arrangement. Another feature which will provide for flexibility is the avoidance of interior bearing walls wherever possible, and the use of concrete block partition walls to act as fire walls and for rodent control. Fire walls which run from basement to roof are barriers to flexibility, and savings in insurance rates may not justify their additional cost. Fire walls at intervals of 100 feet or over are not considered excessive. Stairways leading to basement space should be constructed of concrete or steel and can be as narrow as 3 feet. However, where the basement is to be used for merchandising, a width of not less than 4 to 5 feet should be provided.

3. Second Floors.

In small centers two-story shops are seldom advisable. Second floors do not necessarily increase earnings. Even where additional purchasing power from doctors and their patients is a consideration, the greatly increased cost of special servicing and maintenance of doctors' offices also requires careful consideration. Offices are not desirable in buildings where people live because of children, cooking odors and other conflicting factors.

If second floors are considered advisable, such types of shops as beauty parlors, tailors, dressmakers, photographers, corset shops, gift shops, art shops, and others not depending on display of merchandise should be located there. In some instances merchants may be able to use second floor or basement space if provided with some first floor display space. Second floor window display space has been successfully used on the street fronts and in the corridors.

Stairs to second floors should be easy to climb with intermediate landings. Ceilings for second floors should be 8½ or 9-feet high, and halls, if not too long, should be 5½ to 6-feet wide.

4. Store Sizes.

(a) *Width*. A great deal of money has been wasted by developers and operators alike in adhering arbitrarily to round figures such as 20, 25, or 50 feet in establishing store widths. Study given to the proper desirable widths necessary to accommodate counters, display cases, and aisles reveals that great economies can be realized both in initial store layout and future alteration if other than round figures are used in column and wall spacing.

The following store widths have been recommended by E. W. Tanner, head of the Architectural Department of the J. C. Nichols Company, after 25 years of experience in the design of shop buildings, and after consultation with Walter Schmidt, E. L. Ostendorf, Cyril DeMara, Hugh Potter, Hugh Prather and others:

(1) If a small storeroom is to have cases and counters only on one side, the minimum width should be about 11 to 12 feet.

(2) If the store is to have counter and wall cases on one side and center display table, then not less than 14 to 15 feet should be provided.

(3) If the store is to have counters and wall cases on both sides and an ample customer aisle in center, about 16 to 17 feet should be provided.

(4) If the room is to have cases and counters on both sides and one center line of display tables, the width should be about 21 to 22 feet.

(5) If the room is to have counters and wall cases on both sides and a center sales island without central vertical cases, the width should be from 26 to 28 feet.

(6) If the room is to have cases and counters on both sides, and an island with vertical central cases as well as counters and with space for service between, then the width should be about 29 to 31 feet.

Walter Schmidt, who is an authority in store layout, recommends a column spacing either 17 or 34 feet which permits division into 17 foot stores or variations from this by placing the partition on either side of the column. This arrangement will permit store widths of 10 to 11 feet with wall cases on one side with one counter, 17 feet for wall cases on two sides with a counter, or 22 to 23 feet for wall cases with two counters and a center case.

(b) *Depth.* The ability to provide stores of varying depths is a very valuable asset to any center. Depths from 40 up to 150 feet are required in many cases. It is advisable to use curtain walls in the rear where possible in order to permit future deepening at a minimum of expense. Where it is necessary to construct the building with the same depth throughout, small stores may be "carved out" or be placed on either side of a through corridor. This can be done effectively where double frontage stores are used. Excessive depths from which an adequate return cannot be obtained should, of course, be avoided.

(c) *Flexibility and Cost Saving*. In the discussion on basements and again on store widths and depths, it has been pointed out that flexibility of store space is essential in the successful center. This feature cannot be over-emphasized as adjustment of space for existing tenants to meet their changing needs can then be provided without undue locational shifts. Other methods which promote flexibility include stair wells, electric control boxes, plumbing, heating pipes, and cooling ducts, placed in walls least likely to be removed in enlarging a store. If it is necessary to have them in such walls, they should, if possible, be placed at the extreme rear or extreme front and close together. To provide for future deepening, avoid using the rear wall for this purpose. Where sidewalk grades do not exceed 1 per cent, the first floor can be sloped with the grade to permit two or three stores to be combined later without making changes in floor levels. Store fixtures can readily be adjusted to this slope. Avoid the use of heavy masonry piers between store fronts which reduces window space and is expensive and often difficult to remove at a later date. Front columns should be set back of the front wall from 4 to 6 feet. Small steel columns with curtain walls of gypsum block or exposed painted concrete block are recommended. For one story buildings, steel beam and column construction with steel truss or bar joist roof members carrying light precast concrete slab roof deck, and monolithic concrete floors covered with mastic, terracotta or asphalt tile, permits quick installation, saves labor costs, and provides an incombustible and vermin proof structure.

(d) *Ceiling Heights*. There is a trend toward lower ceiling heights. Modern lighting and air conditioning are factors, together with the savings to be effected initially and in the operation of heating and air conditioning equipment. A majority of the Council believes that in small shops, heights, possibly as low as 9 feet, are permissible. Ten feet has been found to be entirely satisfactory in shops ranging from 10 to 13 feet in width and from 40 to 60 feet deep. These heights should be considered only where the space is not to be combined, as the above heights are too low for large floor areas. False ceilings may, however, be used in certain cases where space is later to be consolidated. In larger shops, ceiling heights of 12 feet are found to be satisfactory. The same ceiling level should be maintained over a considerable area to permit later shop consolidation. Where mezzanines are to be used, a minimum ceiling height of

16 feet is essential. As previously pointed out, basements have been found preferable in many instances for merchandising and offices as well as for storage and toilets and are more economical from a construction and maintenance standpoint. Large store areas may require relatively high ceilings for the sake of appearance to avoid customer resistance. In Westwood Village, Los Angeles, Harold Janss has used a second tier of windows which from the exterior appears to be a second story, but serves in effect as a clearstory on the interior. It should be emphasized that high ceilings increase construction and maintenance costs, and, where located in a two-story building, create resistance to the use of second floors because of long stair runs.

5. Heating and Cooling.

Consideration should be given to space for future cooling plants and ducts even if not immediately provided. It has been found that in one-floor shops, individual heating and cooling plants for each tenant are most satisfactory. Small air conditioning and heating units available at present can take care of individual needs better than a central unit. Where second floors are contemplated, central systems are recommended at the present time. Thermostatic controls to conserve heat should be installed. Central heating plants for buildings of two stories or more should be provided with ample outside air ducts for proper fire combustion.

Oil tanks should be located close to the boiler rooms. Pipes for filling oil tanks should not open at front sidewalks.

If mechanical air conditioning is not provided, there must be good natural ventilation. Skylights may be found desirable in some parts of the country. Unless well designed and constructed, however, they may be a source of cold in winter and heat in summer and subject to breakage and leakage. Careful study should be made of radiator and heating and cooling duct location to avoid interference with the location of store fixtures or partitions which may later be moved. This detail should not be left entirely to heating engineers, contractors or architects.

6. Interiors.

The tendency of customers to walk to the right when entering a store should be recognized in the interior arrangement. It is likely that the best merchandising spot in a store is usually about 1/3 of the way back and on the right-hand side.

Terrazzo or tile floors are most desirable and economical, particularly for drug and food stores and eating places. Masonry floors are recommended over wood in any case. Non-skid floors in halls and stairways are a protection against damage suits.

Generally, too much attention is given to lighting the store interior rather than lighting the merchandise.

D. MANAGEMENT AND MAINTENANCE.

1. Leases.

(a) Percentage leases are believed to be the fairest rental method for both landlord and tenant. The percentage lease arrangement might be looked upon as a form of partnership between the owner of the property on the one hand, and the occupant on the other. The owner furnishes the location and usually the store building, parking space, access, etc.; the tenant supplies the commodities to be marketed. Both are essential to the operation of the business. The skill with which each is done affects its success.

Percentage leases are based upon the ability of the merchant to pay, the kind of business, the volume of business per square foot, the profit made on the merchandise, the importance of the location, absence of too much competition, and similar factors. There are several types of percentage leases. Probably the one most commonly used provides for a minimum guaranteed rental from which the owner will derive enough to cover amortization and operating costs, plus a small return on his investment. This protects both the owner and tenant during possible depression periods. During normal periods of business activity, both parties participate in the increased business, again to their mutual advantage. The usual method is to arrive at the additional rental to be received by the owner by agreeing on a specified percentage of the gross sales. This form is sometimes varied by fixing a maximum rental as well as a minimum, by eliminating both maximum and minimum, or by a sliding scale or "escalator" clause whereby the percentage on the gross sales is increased or reduced as the amount of sales goes up. For example, the lease might stipulate a minimum rental, of say, $5,000; 5 per cent on gross sales from $100,000 to $200,000; 5½ per cent on the next $100,000, and so on. The percentages might be reversed in some cases.

Percentage leases should always give the owner the constant right to check the tenant's books. Accounting should be arranged on a monthly basis if possible. Where tenants have other stores at lower percentage rates or at fixed rentals, the possibility of tenants running sales through those stores must be considered.

It should be emphasized that percentages will vary between various types of merchants in any given shopping center. The tenant should be informed of this to avoid future misunderstanding.

While various percentage ranges and contract forms have been established for different types of stores, they should be considered only as guides. Each case should be considered on its merits, taking into account all of the factors which involve the particular store in question. For this reason it is inadvisable to recommend any particular form of lease contract which would be adaptable to all cases. Unless the developer is thoroughly familiar with percentage lease procedure and practice, he should consult a broker who has specialized in this field.

Percentage leases have become established practice for many types of merchandising and are being extended to others. Cyril DeMara of Toronto, lists the following types of shops which, among others, should pay percentage leases:

"The following are customarily considered percentage lease stores in 100 per cent locations: Five and ten, drug stores, specialty ladies wear, chain restaurants, chain shoes, men's furnishings and hats, hosiery, lingerie and glove stores, nut stores, and candy stores. To this list can normally be added bakeries, ice cream, cafeterias, coffee shops, costume jewelry, cigar stores, department stores, florists, chain groceries, photographic supplies, and shoes. Percentage leases are also being extended to beauty parlors, service shops and many other types. This list may vary, of course, with location and local shopping habits." [1]

[1] For further information on percentage leases the reader is referred to the following published material:

PERCENTAGE LEASES, also CHAIN STORE DIRECTORY, by National Institute of Real Estate Brokers, 22 West Monroe St., Chicago, Illinois.

THE PROBLEMS OF RETAIL SITE LOCATION, by Richard U. Ratcliff, *Michigan Business Studies,* Vol. IX, No. 1, University of Michigan, Ann Arbor, Michigan.

RETAIL STORE LOCATION, by P. D. Converse, in *Opinion and Comment,* Vol. IX, No. 2, May 17, 1947, University of Illinois.

PERCENTAGE LEASES IN TOMORROW'S MARKET, by Stanley L. McMichael, Series beginning in July 1947 issue of *National Real Estate & Building Journal,* Vol. 48, No. 7.

The advice and assistance of Mark Levy, Chicago, in furnishing material upon which this section is based is gratefully acknowledged.

Figure 27.
PERCENTAGE LEASE TABLE, 1947

Compiled annually by the Journal through the aid of its "Board of Experts" composed of George J. Beggs of Norris, Beggs & Simpson, Portland and San Francisco; Frank S. Slosson of Chicago; H. Clifford Bangs of Washington, D. C.; and Harry S. Campbell of Vought, Campbell, Ward & Nicholls, New York City.

TYPE OF STORE	Bangs	Beggs	Slosson	Campbell
Art Shops	7—9	8—10	8—10	8—10
Auto Accessories	6—8	6—8	7—10	5—7
Auto Agencies	3—4	1½—2	3—4	3—4
Bakeries	6—8	5—6	6—8	6—8
Barber Shops	12—15	10	10—15	15
Beauty Shops (Merchandise)	10—12	10	10—15	——
Beauty Shops (Service)	to 20	10—15	15—20	15
Beer Parlors		8	——	8
Books and Stationery	8—10	10	10—12	10—12
Books, Second Hand	10—12	12	12—15	——
Candy	8—10	10—12	8—10	9—10
Candy (with Luncheon)				8—10
Cigars and Tobacco	5—6	6—7	5—7	5—6
Cleaning and Dyeing	8—10	8		8
Cocktail Lounge	8—10	8	8—10	8—10
Credit Clothing	5—7	5—8	6—8	5—6
Department Stores	3—4	2½—4	3—5	3—3¾
Drug Stores (Chain)	4—6	4—7	5—7	6—8
Drug Stores (Individual)	7	7—10	8—10	8—10
Electrical Goods	6—8	5—6	5—7	8—10
Florists	12	7—8	10—12	10—15
Fruit Stores	10—15	——	12—15	10
Fruits and Vegetables	8—10	6	12—15	10
Furs	8—10	7—8	8—10	8—10
Furniture	6—7	5—6	6—8	6—8
Furniture (Credit)	5—6	5—7	6—8	4—7
Garage (Storage)	——	storage 45 sales 10	40—50	40
Gas Stations	1—1½c gal.	5 or 1c gal.	1c gal. gas 1c qt. oil	1—1½c gal.
Grocery Stores (Ordinary)	6	3—5	5—6	3—5
Grocery Stores (Chain)	2—3	2—3	2½—4	2—3
Hardware	6—8	5—7	6—8	6—8
Hosiery and Knit Goods	8—10	7—10	8—10	10
Jewelry	6—8	8—10	10—12	10—12
Jewelry (Cheap Costume)	10—15	10	12	12
Jewelry (Exclusive)	5—6	8—10	10—15	12—15
Linens	10—12	10	10—15	10—12
Liquor Stores	6—8	——	7—9	7—8
Meat Markets	5—6	4—5	6—6	5—7
Meat Markets (Chain)	4—5	——	4—6	4—6
Men's Clothing	5—7	4½—6	6—8	5—7
Men's Furnishings	10	7—8	8—11	10
Men's Hats	7—9	7—8	8—12	8—10
Men's Shoes	6—8	6—8	6—9	7—8
Men's Shoes (Volume)	5—6	5—6	6—8	6—8
Men's Tailors	6—7	6—8	7—9	
Millinery	10—12	12½—15	12—15	10—15
Motion Pictures	12—15	12½—15	12½—25	15—20
Optical Stores	10—15	8—10	10—12	10—12
Paint, Wallpaper Supplies	——	5—6	10	——
Parking Lots	40	40—50	40—50	30—40
Pianos and Musical Instruments	6—8	5—7	7—9	10
Radios	5—7	6	6—9	8
Radios and Electrical	6—8	5—7	6—8	8
Restaurants	8—10	5—9	7—9	8—9
Cafeterias	6—7	7—8	7—8	7—8
Luncheonettes	8—10	8	8—10	8—10
Tea Rooms	8—10	5—8	10	10
Specialty Stores (Non-Advertising)	7—8	8—10		8—10
Sporting Goods	7	6—7	8—10	7—9
Theatres (Combination Vaudeville and Motion Pictures)	——	——	——	12—15
Trunks and Leather Goods	6—8	8—10	8—10	10
Women's Cloaks and Suits	7—8	6—8	6—8	6—8
Women's Cotton Wear	——	7	8—10	8
Women's Furnishings	7—9	6—8	8—10	8—10
Women's Shoes	8—10	6—7	8—10	7—8
Women's Shoes (Volume)	6—8	6—8	6—8	6—8
5-10c or 25c-$2 Stores	5—7	4—6	5—7	5—6

Where fixed rentals are involved, it may be wise for the shopping center owner to investigate the possibility of getting shorter term leases than where the lease is on a percentage basis. On a fixed basis the owner is at a disadvantage in that he is not properly protected as to reasonable increase in rents if he proceeds to develop and expand his center to serve a larger trade area. Also, if it is his policy to limit the number of competing merchants, he is better able to protect himself with a short term fixed lease, and is thereby able to adjust his rent in line with the expansion of the center, limitation on competing stores, or both.

(b) Reasonable protection should be given to merchants from undue competition. However, customers like competitive shops and more than one eating place, dress shop or other types may be desirable. To protect merchants against undue competition, it is therefore necessary to designate in leases the general types of merchandise each will be permitted to sell.

(c) Leases should require, if possible, certain hours for stores to be open so that there is a uniform opening and closing time for the maximum number of merchants. A few dark stores can injure trade in the adjacent stores. It is desirable to require stores that profit thereby, to remain open one or two nights a week, when certain nights can be agreed upon.

(d) Leases should prohibit sidewalk display of merchandise. Window advertising should also be regulated so that gaudy posters and masses of sales placards will not cheapen the entire shopping center.

Encourage tenants to use the name of the shopping center in advertising, and on letterheads and statements.

(e) There should be complete control of awning color and design, but the lease should require all maintenance to be paid by the tenant. All tenants should be required to raise awnings at night.

(f) Exterior signs should also be regulated in the lease contract. No roof or projecting signs should be permitted. Size of lettering and color should be subject to approval by the developer. Letters 12-inches high are considered adequate to be read from 600 feet away without being objectionable. Exterior neon signs are not desirable unless carefully controlled both as to size and color. Paper window signs should not be permitted.

(g) Leases should not be made for too long a period. Except for tenants who make large expenditures on fixtures, it may be necessary to adjust space, adding space for the successful merchant and decreasing it for others. Long leases should not be made for filling stations and "Drive-in" eating places so as to permit change in location.

(h) Leases for food stores, drug stores, bakeries, restaurants and certain other types should provide strict measures for rodent control. Rat-proof refuse receptacles should be provided or required in the rear of such shops.

Broken window glass should be the tenants' reponsibility except when caused by faulty building construction, fire, tornado or explosion covered by the developer's insurance.

Leases should require parking of the tenants' and employees' cars at designated places. This is most important.

2. Management of Parking Areas.

It is recommended that parking areas be provided free and that store rentals be sufficient to cover cost of operation and maintenance. Merchants' Associations sometimes handle maintenance.

If permitted in the center, large offices and organizations using all day parking should be located at the edges of the center with separate parking lots.

3. Maintenance.

Do not underestimate the costs of maintenance and the factor of obsolescence in shopping centers. This cost may be as high as 10 per cent of the rental income. On the other hand, do not underestimate the value of maintaining clean, neat, and attractive surroundings as a patronage builder.

Individual trash incinerators have been found difficult to control and maintain. Provision should be made for temporary fireproof storage of trash inside the building with frequent community pick-up service.

General exterior lighting of buildings is desirable. This may be done by the developer, with the cost assessed to the tenants. Tenants on first floors should have individual water and electric meters. In large buildings master meters may be used and tenants billed by the developer on a pro-rated basis.

All meters should be accessible at all times. Heavy duty hardware, electrical equipment and plumbing fixtures are good investments. Allow ample storage for janitor supplies. Provide ample space for general maintenance and supply quarters.

Cost of maintenance of office space for doctors and dentists is often underestimated and has been found to run twice as high for janitor service alone. Such office standards are high, and new types of medical equipment require expensive changes in wiring and plumbing. Elevators to a second floor medical office are desirable, but they can not be justified unless there is a large number of offices.

There are certain maintenance costs, found by experience, which should be borne directly by the tenant. These include water, heat, light, awning maintenance, and similar items. Interior maintenance, including repainting, should insofar as possible be the responsibility of the tenant. Experience shows that better care is taken of the premises under this arrangement.

Hugh Potter states that one of the most workable ways of clearly defining the responsibility between lessor (landlord) and lessee (tenant) is to insert in the lease a clause providing that the lessor is obligated to maintain the outside of the building, including the roof and structural soundness, while the lessee is obligated to maintain the inside of the leased property, including all doors, windows, and screens.

4. Merchants Associations.

In large shopping centers, merchants' associations can be effective in promoting cooperation among merchants, better municipal service, better transportation, show window contests, joint advertising, seasonal decorations, referring of business, providing night watchmen, trash collection, keeping sidewalks, alleys, and parking stations clean, and similar functions.

Benefits of an association are great to both tenants and the community as a whole. Recommended procedure is the organization of the first merchants in any new center initiated by the developer. This will promote unified action from the beginning which must be continually encouraged. It may be desirable to require membership and collect association dues with the rent. The developer himself should contribute liberally to a merchants' association.

Experience with merchants' associations indicates that, aside from stipulating in the lease that the tenant shall be a member, the organization and operation of the association should be left largely to the merchants to be handled on a voluntary basis. Maintenance assessments based on the front feet of store or square feet of space occupied have not proved practical, as volume of business, possible profit, dependence on off-street parking space, limitation of competition, superiority of location, etc., varies with the type of shop rather than with its space requirements.

A successful method of handling this matter has been worked out in the Country Club Plaza where the directors of the association appoint a representative committee each year composed of seven members which, after careful study of each merchant's requirements, arrives at an annual amount for each establishment which represents its fair share of the expenses of the association. These amounts may vary from as little as $1 per month for certain professional offices to $25 for the larger establishments. In the case of branch department stores, this may be as high as several hundred dollars. With a tenant's increase or decrease in space requirements or volume of business, the commitee will review the case and make adjustments accordingly. The company as landlord contributes one quarter of the total amount collected by the association. The Plaza Association maintains an office furnished by the company with two full-time employees, one of whom acts as a public relations and contact man with new residents in the area. In addition, two maintenance men are employed to help keep sidewalks, streets, parking stations, lawn and park areas clean. This type of operation has proved highly successful and the few objections to assessments levied by the committee have been agreeably settled within the organization.

In smaller centers it is, of course, not always possible for the merchants to maintain a staff, but an organization should be set up and their activities geared to the size and nature of the center. Much can be accomplished by this type of group effort where the center operates as a unit.

The following are some of the activities of merchants' associations:

1. Conduct general center advertising campaigns.
2. Prizes for window displays.
3. Encouragement of common night opening dates.
4. Referral of customers to the proper stores within the center for their purchases.
5. Publication of a news bulletin.
6. Semi-monthly luncheon meeting.
7. Merchants' directory for public distribution.
8. Check on advertising solicitations.

9. Calling on new residents.
10. Developing employees' interest.
11. Collective trash hauling.
12. Keeping sidewalks clean.
13. Snow removal.
14. Promoting united Christmas and other seasonal events and decorations.
15. Acquainting merchants with each other and encouraging friendly relations.
16. Enforcing parking regulations—a very important function.
17. Many other activities can be effectively performed by a good merchants' association as the occasion warrants.

Besides the board of directors, various committees can work for better transportation, adequate street lighting and police protection, and similar items. It has been found that an association is frequently more effective in these matters than the landlord.

5. The Shopping Center Customer.

It may be well to point out for final general consideration that the suburban shopping center customer expects and demands more freedom and less restrictions and regulations than he will willingly accept in the downtown central business district. He or usually she, wishes to feel free to bring the baby, to come on a bicycle, or in shorts, house dress or other informal attire. She wishes to be able to visit with friends on the street or in the shop, take more time for lunch, park her car as she wishes. Customers object to one-way streets and parking meters. These habits and wishes should be given every possible consideration in designing the center. It is a natural outcome of the neighborhood environment and one of the reasons why neighborhood centers are becoming increasingly popular. Every effort should be made by the developer to promote this atmosphere.

Concluding Statement

In this volume the Community Builders' Council has attempted to record the conclusions and suggestions which have been developed collectively through its deliberations on the subject of Community Development, and which, in turn, are the result of the extensive individual experience of its members in this field. The Council is convinced that through the application of these principles to community development, more permanent, attractive, and stable residential and commercial areas will result in our cities which will be directly reflected in sounder, more durable health, social, financial, and civic values.

In this process, the Council urges the greatest cooperation and consultation with the public officials and departments of the local governments who represent the community. In turn, it is urged that these officials and departments give serious attention to the multitude of problems which confront the community builder in his undertaking, and with which obviously they can not always be fully acquainted. It is the hope of the Council that many of the practical considerations which must govern new community development have been pointed out. Community building as a cooperative undertaking cannot be solved by unduly rigid, extravagant, and drastic public regulations without greatly hampering the potentialities of the development itself and the city as a whole. It is through this kind of reciprocal cooperation that the fullest extent of enduring values can be realized.

American cities have been notorious for the vast losses which occur each decade in large segments of our urban areas through the building up and tearing down process. Sound community development, built in terms of generations instead of decades, will go far toward helping to remove this destructive process through providing better living environment for our citizens, preventing future slums, and maintaining the stable and reliable taxable values which are so necessary to the financial support of the governmental unit of which the community is a part.

Appendices

Appendix A

PROTECTIVE COVENANTS

Recommended by the Federal Housing Administration

These Covenants are to run with the land and shall be binding on all parties and all persons claiming under them until January 1, 19____, at which time said Covenants shall be automatically extended for successive periods of 10[1] years unless by vote of a majority of the then owners of the lots it is agreed to change said covenants in whole or in part.

If the parties hereto, or any of them, or their heirs or assigns, shall violate or attempt to violate any of the Covenants herein it shall be lawful for any other person or persons owning any real property situated in said development or subdivision to prosecute any proceedings at law or in equity against the person or persons violating or attempting to violate any such Covenant and either to prevent him or them from so doing or to recover damages or other dues for such violation.

Invalidation of any one of these Covenants by judgment or court order shall in no wise affect any of the other provisions which shall remain in full force and effect.

A All lots in the tract shall be known and described as residential lots, except _____

_____

(Describe areas to be designated in separate covenant for retail business, schools, churches, etc.)

No structures shall be erected, altered, placed or permitted to remain on any residential building plot other than one detached single-family dwelling or one _____ dwelling not to

(Semi-detached single-family, etc.)

exceed two and one-half stories in height and a private garage for not more than ____ cars and _____

_____

(Other outbuildings incidental to residential use of the plot)

B No building shall be erected, placed, or altered on any building plot in this subdivision until the building plans, specifications, and plot plan showing the location of such building have been approved in writing as to conformity and harmony of external design with existing structures in the subdivision, and as to location of the building with respect to topography and finished ground elevation, by a committee composed of _____, _____ and _____, or by a representative designated by a majority of the members of said committee. In the event of death or resignation of any member of said committee, the remaining member, or members, shall have full authority to approve or disapprove such design and location, or to designate a representative with like authority. In the event said committee, or its designated representative, fails to approve or disapprove such design and location within 30 days after said plans and specifications have been submitted to it or, in any event, if no suit to enjoin the erection of such building or the making of such alterations has been commenced prior to the completion thereof,

---

[1] Some developers recommend not less than 25 years.

such approval will not be required and this Covenant will be deemed to have been fully complied with. Neither the members of such committee, nor its designated representative shall be entitled to any compensation for services performed pursuant to this Covenant. The powers and duties of such committee, and of its designated representative, shall cease on and after _____. Thereafter the approval described in this Covenant shall not be required unless, prior to said date and effective thereon, a written instrument shall be executed by the then record owners of a majority of the lots in this subdivision and duly recorded appointing a representative, or representatives, who shall thereafter exercise the same powers previously exercised by said committee.

Note.—Covenant B may be omitted provided harmony of external design and location is otherwise assured to the satisfaction of the Federal Housing Administration.

C No building shall be located nearer to the front lot line or nearer to the side street line than the building setback lines shown on the recorded plat. In any event, no building shall be located on any residential building plot nearer than ____ feet to the front lot line, nor nearer than ____ feet to any side street line; except that on all building plots abutting _____, no building shall be located nearer than _____ feet to the front lot line nor nearer than _____ feet to any side street line. No building, except detached garage or other outbuilding located _____ feet or more from the front lot line, shall be located nearer than _____ feet to any side lot line.

Note.—The building setback lines to be shown on the recorded plat shall be as described in C. Exceptions to setback lines, applying to entire tract or to certain lots, may be made in C where special conditions warrant. If desired a maximum setback line may be included as follows:

No residence or attached appurtenance shall be erected on any lot farther than _____ feet from the front lot line.

D No residential structure shall be erected or placed on any building plot, which plot has an area of less than _____ square feet or a width of less than _____ feet at the front building setback line, except that a residence may be erected or placed on lots Nos. _____ _____ as shown on the recorded plat.

E No noxious or offensive trade or activity shall be carried on upon any lot nor shall anything be done thereon which may be or become an annoyance or nuisance to the neighborhood.

F No trailer, basement, tent, shack, garage, barn, or other outbuilding erected in the tract shall at any time be used as a residence temporarily or permanently, nor shall any structure of a temporary character be used as a residence.

G No dwelling costing less than $_____ shall be permitted on any lot in the tract. The ground floor area of the main structure, exclusive of one-story open porches and garages, shall be not less than _____ square feet in the case of a one-story structure nor less than _____ square feet in the case of a one and one-half, two, or two and one-half story structure.

H-1 Easements affecting lot Nos. _____ _____ are reserved as shown on the recorded plat, for utility installation and maintenance.

168

H-2 An easement is reserved over the rear 5 feet of each lot for utility installation and maintenance.

NOTE.—Utility easements should be provided only where needed. Include clause H-1 or H-2, depending upon the method to be used. *Additional covenants to meet special conditions shall be added here.*

ADDITIONAL PROTECTIVE COVENANTS

Recommended by Federal Housing Administration

.(Special Condition A- Add to C to permit garages to be located nearer the street on approval of the Property Owners' Committee.) Excepting as otherwise provided or controlled by law and with written approval of the Property Owners' Committee, private one-story attached garages may be located nearer to the street line than the established building lines, but not nearer than _____ feet to any street line, where the natural grade of the lot at the established building line is more than either eight feet above or four feet below the average established roadway level of the street on which the lot abuts, on condition that the floor level of such attached garage shall be not more than one foot above the established roadway grade of the street.

(Special Condition B- Add to C to authorize the Property Owners' Committee to permit variation from setback lines.) On Lot Nos. _____ _____ a reasonable variation from established building lines may be authorized by the Property Owners' Committee referred to above, in order to conform to existing physical conditions on the lot or its surroundings, *provided* that no building may be located nearer than _____ feet to any street line.

I Lot Nos. _____ may be
used for _____·
(Retail, business, schools, churches, etc.)

However, by vote of the then owners of the majority of such lots as of January 1, 19____, residences may be constructed or moved onto these lots provided that lots so improved are either contiguous to lots containing existing dwellings or to lots designated in Paragraph A for residential use, and further provided that such lots front or abut the same street or streets on which the aforesaid residential lots front or abut, and provided that such residences are not more than three stories in height and cover not more than _____ per cent of the building plot. The location with respect to the side lot line of all buildings on the lots designated in this covenant shall be determined by the Property Owners' Committee except as may be otherwise indicated on the recorded plat.

J Until such time as a sanitary sewer system shall have been constructed to serve _____ (*"this subdivision" or specified lots*) _____, a sewage disposal system constructed in accordance with the requirements of the _____ shall be installed to
(Health authority with jurisdiction)
serve each dwelling. The effluent from septic tanks shall not be permitted to discharge into a stream, storm sewer, open ditch or drain, un-

less it has been first passed through an absorption field approved by the health authority.

K Until such time as water is available from a semi-public or municipal system to serve _____ (*"this subdivision" or specified lots*) _____ _____, an adequate supply of water shall be secured from approved sources located, constructed, and equipped in accordance with local and state regulations, and no means of water supply shall be permitted unless such supply has the written approval of the _____.

(Health authority having jurisdiction)

L Both private or semi-public water supply and sewage disposal systems may be located on the same building plot or within or adjacent to this subdivision to serve any building plot in the subdivision *provided* written approval has been given by the health authority having jurisdiction, stating that such water supply and sewage disposal systems are satisfactory to serve all lots, taking into consideration the conditions and hazards which can reasonably be expected to exist when all lots to which these covenants apply have been built up with houses or _____ similarly served, and further provided that (a) no septic tank shall be closer than _____ feet and no cesspool or tile absorption field shall be closer than _____ feet to a dwelling, _____ feet to a well, _____ feet to a stream, or _____ feet to a property line, or where the surface or ground water flow is toward the well or dwelling, and an absorption field not less than _____ feet in length of open joint agricultural tile shall be provided, laid at a grade of not more than _____ inches in _____ feet, not more than _____ inches below the surface of the ground, and the lines not less than _____ feet apart and (b) no leaching cesspool shall be located nearer to a dwelling than _____ feet or nearer to a well than _____ feet.

M No fence, wall, hedge, or mass planting shall be permitted to extend nearer to any street than the minimum building setback line except that nothing shall prevent the erection of a necessary retaining wall, the top of which does not extend more than ____ feet above the finished grade at the back of said retaining wall.

N No building shall be placed nor shall any material or refuse be placed or stored on any lot within 20 feet of the property line of any park or edge of any open water course, *except* that clean fill may be placed nearer to the lot line provided the natural water course is not altered or blocked by such fill.

O Oil drilling, oil development operations, or refining, or mining operations of any kind, or quarrying shall not be permitted upon or in any of the lots in the tract described herein, nor shall oil wells, tanks, tunnels, mineral excavations or shafts be permitted upon or in any of the lots within the subdivision.

P The owner of each building plot to which these covenants apply shall be entitled to one membership in a cooperative _____

(Water system, road maintenance, etc.)

association and to participate in the operation of the system in accordance with the by-laws of said association filed herewith.

170

Appendix B

Sample Form

PROTECTIVE COVENANTS

Conditions, Covenants, Restrictions, and Easements Affecting Property of the _____ Corporation.

THIS DECLARATION, made this _____ day of _____, by the _____ Corporation, hereinafter called the Declarant,

WITNESSETH:

WHEREAS, Declarant is the owner of the real property described in Clause I of this Declaration, and is desirous of subjecting the real property described in said Clause I to the restrictions, covenants, reservations, easements, liens and charges hereinafter set forth, each and all of which is and are for the benefit of said property and for each owner thereof, and shall inure to the benefit of and pass with said property, and each and every parcel thereof, and shall apply to and bind the successors in interest, and any owner thereof;

Now, THEREFORE, _____ Corporation hereby declares that the real property described in and referred to in Clause I hereof is, and shall be, held, transferred, sold and conveyed subject to the conditions, restrictions, covenants, reservations, easements, liens and charges hereinafter set forth.

Definition of Terms

Building Site shall mean any lot, or portion thereof, or any two or more contiguous lots, or a parcel of land of record and in a single ownership and upon which a dwelling may be erected in conformance with the requirements of these Covenants.

Corporation shall mean the _____ Corporation.

Association shall refer to the Homes Association of the tract covered by these Covenants or any extension thereof as herein provided.

CLAUSE I.

Property Subject to This Declaration

The real property which is, and shall be, held and shall be conveyed, transferred and sold subject to the conditions, restrictions, covenants, reservations, easements, liens and charges with respect to the various portions thereof set forth in the various clauses and subdivisions of this Declaration is located in the County of _____, State of _____, and is more particularly described as follows, to-wit:

(Insert legal description.)

No property other than that described above shall be deemed subject to this Declaration, unless and until specifically made subject thereto.

The declarant may, from time to time, subject additional real property to the conditions, restrictions, covenants, reservations, liens and charges herein set forth by appropriate reference hereto.

171

CLAUSE II.

General Purposes of Conditions

The real property described in Clause I hereof is subjected to the covenants, restrictions, conditions, reservations, liens and charges hereby declared to insure the best use and the most appropriate development and improvement of each building site thereof; to protect the owners of building sites against such improper use of surrounding building sites as will depreciate the value of their property; to preserve, so far as practicable, the natural beauty of said property; to guard against the erection thereon of poorly designed or proportioned structures, and structures built of improper or unsuitable materials; to obtain harmonious color schemes; to insure the highest and best development of said property; to encourage and secure the erection of attractive homes thereon, with appropriate locations thereof on building sites; to prevent haphazard and inharmonious improvement of building sites; to secure and maintain proper setbacks from streets, and adequate free spaces between structures; and in general to provide adequately for a high type and quality of improvement in said property, and thereby to enhance the values of investments made by purchasers of building sites therein.

A All Building sites in the tract shall be known and described as residential building sites, except _____
_____ No
(Describe areas to be designated
in separate covenant for retail business, schools, churches, etc.)
structures shall be erected, altered, placed, or permitted to remain on any building site other than one detached single-family dwelling not to exceed two and one-half stories in height, a private garage for not more than three cars, guest house, servants' quarters, and other outbuildings incidental to residential use of the premises.

B No building shall be erected, placed, or altered on any premises in said development until the building plans, specifications, and plot plan showing the location of such building have been approved in writing as to conformity and harmony of external design with existing structures in the development, and as to location of the building with respect to topography and finished ground elevation, by an architectural committee composed of _____, _____, and
_____, or by a representative designated by a majority of the members of said committee. In the event of death or resignation of any member of said committee, the remaining member, or members, shall have full authority to approve or disapprove such design and location, or to designate a representative with like authority. In the event said committee, or its designated representative, fails to approve or disapprove such design and location within 30 days after said plans and specifications have been submitted to it or, in any event, if no suit to enjoin the erection of such building or the making of such alterations has been commenced prior to the completion thereof, such approval will not be required and this Covenant will be deemed to have been fully complied with. Neither the members of such committee, nor its designated representative shall be entitled to any compensation for services performed pursuant to this Covenant.

172

C No building shall be located on any building site less than _____ feet from the front lot line for all sites covered by these covenants, nor less than _____ feet from any side street line. No building shall be located less than _____ feet from any side lot line or _____ feet from any building on the same site, except a detached garage or other outbuilding located in the rear yard may be placed _____ feet from the side line. No residence shall be so located as to reduce the rear yard of the plot on which it is located to less than _____ feet.

D No residential structure shall be erected or placed on any building site, which has an area of less than _____ square feet or a width of less than _____ feet at the front building setback line for interior lots, and less than _____ feet for corner lots.

E No noxious or offensive trade or activity shall be carried on upon any building site nor shall anything be done thereon which may be or become an annoyance or nuisance to the neighborhood.

F No trailer, basement, tent, shack, garage, barn, or other outbuilding other than guest houses and servants' quarters erected on a building site covered by these Covenants shall at any time be used for human habitation temporarily or permanently, nor shall any structure of a temporary character be used for human habitation.

G No main residential structure shall be permitted on any building site covered by these covenants, the habitable floor area of which, exclusive of basements, porches, and garages, is less than _____ square feet in the case of a one-story structure or less than _____ square feet in the case of a one and one-half, two, or two and one-half story structure.

H Where no alleys are provided, an easement is hereby reserved over the rear five feet of each building site for utility installation and maintenance.

I No animals or poultry of any kind other than house pets shall be kept or maintained on any part of said property.

J The premises hereby conveyed shall not be occupied, leased, rented, conveyed or otherwise alienated, nor shall the title or possession thereof pass to another without the written consent of the Grantor, except that the Grantor shall not withhold such consent if and after a written consent is given to permit such occupation, leasing, renting, conveyance or alienation by a majority of the owners of the fifteen (15) building sites included within these covenants most immediately adjacent to the said premises, and which adjoin or face said premises for a distance of five (5) building sites from the respective side lines of said premises, and also the five (5) building sites which are most immediately adjacent thereto and across any street upon which said premises front; except transfer of title by way of devise or inheritance, in which case the devisee or heir shall take such property subject to the restrictions herein imposed, and except that said property may be mortgaged or subjected to judicial sale, provided, in any such case, that no purchaser of said premises at judicial sale shall have the right to occupy, lease, rent, convey or otherwise alienate said premises without the written consent of the Grantor first had and obtained in the manner above stated.

In the event there is a total of less than fifteen (15) building sites which meet the consent requirements of this Section, then a sufficient number of the most immediately adjacent building sites included within these covenants and lying to the rear of said premises shall be included to obtain the required fifteen (15) building sites.

It is understood, however, that the rights hereby reserved to the Grantor shall apply with equal force and effect to its successors and assigns; but in the event the ownership and control of the rights hereby reserved, pass from the hands of the Corporation, either by reason of the appointment of a Receiver, assignment for the benefit of creditors, bankruptcy, by sale under legal process of any kind, by the transfer of the ownership of a majority stock to other than the Corporation's interests, or otherwise, the provision for consents by the Grantor in this Section J, provided for, shall be deemed to be sufficiently obtained when obtained only from a majority of the owners of the said adjoining and facing building sites, as specified in Section J herein, and thenceforth the right to enforce the restrictions in this Section J of this deed contained shall immediately pass to the said owners of the said adjoining and facing building sites.

K No fence, wall, hedge, or mass planting shall be permitted to extend beyond the minimum building setback line established herein except upon approval by the architectural committee as provided in Section B.

L Oil drilling, oil development operations; refining, mining operations of any kind, or quarrying shall not be permitted upon or in any of the building sites in the tract described herein, nor shall oil wells, tanks, tunnels, mineral excavations or shafts be permitted upon or in any of the building sites covered by these Covenants.

M The owner of each building site to which these covenants apply shall be entitled to one membership in a Homes Association and to participate in the operation of the Association in accordance with the by-laws of said Association filed herewith.

N These Covenants are to run with the land and shall be binding on all parties and all persons claiming under them until January 1, 19___, (twenty-five year period), at which time said Covenants shall be automatically extended for successive periods of 10[1] years unless by vote of a majority of the then owners of the building sites covered by these covenants it is agreed to change said covenants in whole or in part.

If the parties hereto, or any of them, or their heirs or assigns, shall violate or attempt to violate any of the Covenants herein, it shall be lawful for any other person or persons owning any real property situated in said tract, or the Homes Association as provided in Section M, to prosecute any proceedings at law or in equity against the person or persons violating or attempting to violate any such Covenant, and either to prevent him or them from so doing or to recover damages or other dues for such violation.

O Invalidation of any one of these Covenants or any part thereof by judgments or court order shall in no wise affect any of the other provisions which shall remain in full force and effect.

---

[1] Some developers recommend as high as a 40 year initial period with successive extensions of 25 years.

Appendix C

Sample Form

DECLARATION OF INCORPORATION

OF

_____ HOMES ASSOCIATION

This declaration made on this _____ day of _____ 19__, by _____, a corporation of the State of _____, the owner of property set opposite its name below, and those individuals whose names are subscribed hereto as the owners of the lots set opposite their respective names.

WITNESSETH: That whereas, _____ Corporation is now developing parts of said _____ for high class residential
(Subdivision)
purposes, and it is the desire to continue the development of certain parts of such land and other land in this vicinity for such purposes, and for the creation and maintenance of a residential community possessing features of more than ordinary value to a residential community, and

WHEREAS, In order to assist it and its grantees in providing the necessary means to better enable it and its grantees to bring this about, the parties hereto do now and hereby subject all of the property, described below to the following covenants, charges and assessments.

KNOW ALL MEN BY THESE PRESENTS:
That we, the undersigned, have this day voluntarily associated ourselves together for the purpose of forming a non-profit corporation under the laws of the State of _____, and we do hereby certify:

SECTION 1. That the name of this corporation is:

"_____" HOMES ASSOCIATION

SECTION 2. That this corporation, hereafter referred to as the Association, is a corporation which does not contemplate pecuniary gain or profit to the members thereof, and that the purposes for which it is formed are:

(a) To exercise its powers and functions on the following described real property situated in the Town of _____, _____ County, State of _____, and more particularly described as follows:
All of the real property shown on that certain map entitled, "_____", _____ County, _____, filed in the office of the Town Clerk of the Town of _____ on _____ __, ____.
(Date)

Together with any and all other real property which may hereafter, through the operation of conditions, covenants, restrictions, easements, reservations or charges pertaining to the same, be placed under or submitted to the jurisdiction of this Association, and be accepted as within the jurisdiction of this Association by resolution of the Board of Directors of this Association (which said real property hereinabove specifically described, together with the property hereafter within the jurisdiction of this Association as above provided, is referred to as "said property").

(b) To care for vacant, unimproved and unkempt lots in said property, remove and destroy grass, weeds and rodents therefrom, and any unsightly and obnoxious thing therefrom, and to do any other things, and perform any labor necessary or desirable in the judgment of this Association to keep the property, and the land contiguous and adjacent thereto neat and in good order.

(c) To pay the taxes and assessments, if any, which may be levied by any governmental authority upon roads and parks in said property, and any other open spaces maintained, and lands used or acquired for the general use of the owners of lots or building sites within said property, and on any property of this Association, or which may be held in trust for this Association.

(d) To enforce charges, restrictions, conditions and covenants existing upon and created for the benefit of said property over which this Association has jurisdiction; to pay all expenses incidental thereto; to enforce the decisions and rulings of this Association having jurisdiction over any of said property; to pay all of the expenses in connection therewith; and to reimburse any declarant under any declaration of conditions, covenants, restrictions, assessments or charges affecting said property, or any part thereof, for all costs and expenses incurred or paid by it in connection with the enforcement, or attempted enforcement, of any of the conditions, covenants, restrictions, charges, assessments or terms set forth in any declaration.

(e) To provide for the maintenance of tennis courts, playgrounds, water areas and other community features on land set aside for the general use of the members of said Association, and to maintain and operate the country club and golf course in proportion to its percentage of membership therein.

(f) To do any and all lawful things and acts which this Association at any time, and from time to time, shall, in its discretion, deem to be to the best interests of said property and the owners of the building sites thereon, and to pay all costs and expenses in connection therewith.

(g) Any powers and duties exercised by said Association relating to maintenance, operation, construction or reconstruction of any facility provided for herein may be contracted for with the _____ Corporation or other qualified contractor as agent.

(h) To fix the rate per square foot of the annual charges or assessments to which said property shall be made subject; to collect the charges or assessments affecting said property; to pay all expenses in connection therewith, and all office and other expenses incident to the conduct of the business of this Association, and all licenses, franchise taxes, and governmental charges levied or imposed against said property of this Association; such charges or assessments shall become a lien on said property as soon as due and payable. Settlement of such lien shall be made as determined by the Directors of this Association.

176

(i) To acquire by gift, purchase, or otherwise to own, hold, enjoy, lease, operate, maintain, and to convey, sell, lease, transfer, mortgage, or otherwise encumber, dedicate for public use, or otherwise dispose of real or personal property in connection with the business of this Association.

(j) To expend the moneys collected by this Association from assessments or charges and other sums received by this Association for the payment and discharge of all proper costs, expenses and obligations incurred by this Association in carrying out any or all of the purposes for which this Association is formed.

(k) To borrow money; to mortgage, pledge, deed in trust, or hypothecate any or all of its real or personal property as security for money borrowed or debts incurred, and to do any and all things that an association organized under said laws of the State of _____ may lawfully do, and generally to do and perform any and all other acts which may be either necessary for, or proper or incidental to the exercise of any of the foregoing powers, and such powers as are granted by the provisions of the laws of the State of _____ to a non-profit corporation.

(1) To do any and all lawful things which may be advisable, proper, authorized or permitted to be done by this Association under and by virtue of any condition, covenant, restriction, reservation, charge, or assessment affecting said property, or any portion thereof, and to do and perform any and all acts which may be either necessary for or incidental to the exercise of any of the foregoing powers, or for the peace, health, comfort, safety, or general welfare of the owners of said property, or any portion thereof, or residents thereon.[1]

SECTION 3. That the town in this state where the principal office for the transaction of the business of this Association is to be located is the Town of _____, _____ County, _____

SECTION 4. That the number of directors of this Association shall be five; that the names and addresses of the persons who are to act in the capacity of directors until the selection of their successors are as follows:

NAMES   ADDRESSES

That the number of directors, as hereinabove set forth, may be changed by a by-law duly adopted pursuant to authority contained in this Declaration of Incorporation, and authority is hereby granted to change the number of directors by an amendment to the by-laws of this Association which by-laws shall be adopted in accordance with the terms of this declaration.

SECTION 5. The members of this Association shall be:

(a) All persons who are owners of record of any building site in said property, provided that no person or corporation taking title as security for the payment of money or the performance of any obligation shall thereby become entitled to membership.

_____
[1] An additional clause may be added giving the Association general authority to cover other matters as the need may arise.

(b) All persons who reside on a building site in said property, and who are purchasing such building site under a contract or agreement of purchase.

Such ownership or such residence and the purchasing of such building site under a contract or agreement of purchase shall be the only qualifications for membership in this Association.

When a building site is owned of record in joint tenancy or tenancy in common, or when two or more residents are purchasing a building site under a contract or agreement of purchase, the membership as to such building site shall be joint and the right of such membership (including the voting power arising therefrom) shall be exercised only by the joint action of all owners of record of such building site, or of all purchasers under said contract or agreement of purchase, respectively.

Membership in this Association shall lapse and terminate when any member shall cease to be the owner of record of a building site, or upon any member ceasing to be a resident on a building site in said property or a purchaser thereof under a contract or agreement of purchase.

A building site for the purpose of this Declaration of Incorporation shall be taken to be and mean a building site as defined in the protective covenants covering the portion of said property in which the building site is located.

The voting power of members of this Association shall be limited to one vote for each building site, as defined in the covenants covering said property, owned or under purchase contract by such members.[1]

The owner or contract purchaser of any building site which is or may hereafter be included within the jurisdiction of this Association shall be automatically eligible for membership in the _____ Country Club to the extent of two persons for each building site so owned or under contract, without the payment of an initiation fee and including all usual membership privileges. Such owner or contract purchaser shall, however, be personally responsible for any subsequent annual dues, greens fees, or other fees which may be charged in addition to the general assessments levied by said Association. Membership eligibility without payment of an initiation fee shall lapse and terminate when any person or persons shall cease to be an owner of record or a contract purchaser of a building site within the jurisdiction of said Association.[2]

Each member of this Association shall have such interest in all the property owned by this Association as is represented by the ratio of the number of votes in this Association. Such interest is and shall be appurtenant to the building sites which qualify such person for membership in this Association.

---

[1] Certain difficulties may arise from this method of representation. Some developers advocate giving only one vote to each owner, including the developer, regardless of the amount of land or number of sites he may hold. This is probably a more democratic method and subject to less misinterpretation. Each developer should decide this question on the basis of his own project and experience.

[2] Clauses referring to the country club should be included only where it is desired that this facility, if provided in the development, be under the Homes Association.

In Witness Whereof, for the purpose of forming this Association under the laws of the State of _____, we, the undersigned, constituting the incorporators of this Association, including the persons hereinabove named as the first directors of this Association, have executed this Declaration of Incorporation this _____ day of _____, 19___.

Signed: _____

_____

_____

_____

_____

The above clauses are designed to fit areas in which municipal authority furnishes most or all of the municipal services. If the development lies in an area where municipal services are not provided, or plan approval is to be included, additional clauses similar to the following should be added under Section 2:

(1) To improve, light, provide for, beautify, and maintain streets, parks, and other open spaces, including all grass plots, park strips, other planted areas and trees and shrubs within the lines of said streets in and bordering upon said property as shall be maintained for public use, or for the general use of the owners of lots or building sites in said property, but only until such time as such services are adequately provided by public authority.

(2) To sweep, clean and sprinkle the streets within and bordering upon and adjacent to said property; to collect and dispose of street sweepings, garbage, rubbish, and the like from said property; to provide for community police and fire protection of said property, and to construct, maintain and keep in repair fire hydrants and mains, sewers, and any sewage disposal systems, but only until such time as such services are adequately provided for by public authority.

(3) To pay for the examination and approval, or disapproval, of plans, specifications, color schemes, block plans and grading plans for any building, outhouse, garage, stable, fence, wall, retaining wall, or other structure of any kind which shall be erected, constructed, placed or maintained on said property, or any part thereof, and for any alteration, condition, changing, repairing, remodeling, or adding to the exterior thereof, and for such supervision of construction and inspection as may be required to insure compliance therewith, including the services of architects and other persons employed to examine and advise upon such plans, specifications, color schemes, block plans, and grading plans.

If it is desired to define the voting and property rights and interests of members of the association in more detail, clauses should be added similar to those in Article III of Association By-Laws, page 181.

Appendix D

Sample Form

BY-LAWS

OF

_____ HOMES ASSOCIATION

ARTICLE I.

Definitions

Section 1—The words "said property" as used in these By-Laws shall be deemed to mean the following described real property situated in the County of _____, State of _____, and more particularly described as follows:

All of the real property shown on that certain map entitled, "_____" filed in the office of the County Recorder of the County of _____, State of _____, on _____ _____, _____, in Map Book _____.
(Date)

Together with any and all other real property which may hereafter, through the operation of conditions, covenants, restrictions, easements, reservations or charges pertaining to the same, be placed under or submitted to the jurisdiction of this corporation and be accepted as within the jurisdiction of this corporation by resolution of the Board of Directors of this corporation.

Section 2—The words "building site" wherever used in these By-Laws shall be deemed to mean a building site as defined in any declaration of conditions, covenants, restrictions, easements, reservations or charges affecting the portion of said property in which the building site is located.

ARTICLE II.

Membership

Section 1—The members of this corporation shall be:

(a) All persons who are owners of record of any building site in said property, provided that no person or corporation taking title as security for the payment of money or the performance of any obligation shall thereby become entitled to membership.

(b) All persons who reside on a building site in said property, and who are purchasing such building site under a contract or agreement of purchase.

Such ownership or such residence and the purchasing of such building site under a contract or agreement of purchase shall be the only qualifications for membership in this corporation.

When a building site is owned of record in joint tenancy or tenancy in common, or when two or more residents are purchasing a building site under a contract or agreement of purchase, the membership as to such building site shall be joint and the right of such membership (including the voting power arising therefrom) shall be exercised only by the joint action of all owners of record of such building site, or of all purchasers under said contract or agreement of purchase, respectively.

Any person claiming to be a member in this corporation shall establish his right to membership to the satisfaction of the Secretary of this corporation. No membership or initiation fee shall be charged, nor shall members be required to pay at any time any amount to carry on the business of this corporation, except to pay annually the charges or assessments set forth in the declaration of conditions, covenants, restrictions, easements and charges dated the _____ day of _____, _____, executed by _____ Company, and recorded on the _____ day of _____, _____, in the office of the County Recorder of the County of _____, State of _____, in Volume _____ of Official Records at page _____ thereof, or as set forth in any other declaration affecting any portion of said property.

Membership in this corporation shall lapse and terminate when any member shall cease to be the owner of record of a building site, or upon any member ceasing to be a resident on a building site in said property and a purchaser thereof under a contract or agreement of purchase.

ARTICLE III.
Voting Rights

Section 1—In all matters which shall come before the members of this corporation, and in all corporate matters, the voting power of the members of this corporation shall be unequal, according to the following rules:

(a) Except as provided in (d) of this section, each member of this corporation shall have at least one vote.

(b) Except as provided in (d) of this section, each member of this corporation owning of record one or more building sites shall have the right to the number of votes equal to the total number of building sites of which he is the owner of record.[1]

(c) Except as provided in (d) of this section, each purchaser who is a resident on a building site and is purchasing it under a contract or agreement of purchase shall be entitled to one vote.

(d) When a building site is owned of record in joint tenancy or tenancy in common, or when two or more residents are purchasing a building site under a contract or agreement of purchase and residing thereon, the several owners or purchasers of said building site shall collectively be entitled to one vote only therefor.

ARTICLE IV.
Property Rights

Section 1—Each member of this corporation shall have such an interest in all of the property owned by this corporation as is represented by the ratio of the number of votes to which said member is

---
[1] See footnote 1 on page 178.

entitled to the total number of votes in this corporation. Such interest is and shall be appurtenant to the building sites in all said property which qualify such person for membership in this corporation.

ARTICLE V.

Corporate Powers

Section 1—The corporate powers of this corporation shall be vested in, exercised by, and under the authority of, and the business and affairs of this corporation shall be controlled by a board of five directors. The directors, other than those named in the Articles of Incorporation shall be members of the corporation. Three of said directors shall constitute a quorum for the transaction of business.

ARTICLE VI.

Election of Directors

Section 1—The directors named in the Articles of Incorporation of this corporation shall hold office until the next annual meeting thereafter and until their successors are elected, either at an annual meeting or at a special meeting called for that purpose, unless otherwise provided by the By-Laws of this corporation.

Section 2—Unless otherwise provided by the By-Laws of this corporation, the Directors, other than those named in the Articles of Incorporation, shall be elected at the annual meeting of the members, and shall hold office until their successors are elected.

Section 3—Unless otherwise provided by the By-Laws of this corporation, the term of office of any director shall begin immediately after election. The term of office of members of the Board of Directors of this corporation may be determined by a majority of the members of this corporation and may, from time to time, be changed if demanded in writing by a majority of the members of this corporation.

Section 4—Upon the sale of fifty-one per cent (51%) of the building sites shown on that certain map entitled, _____ _____ filed in the office of the County Recorder of the County of _____, State of _____ on _____, in Map Book _____ at pages
                    (Date)
_____ inclusive, as said building sites are defined in that certain Declaration of conditions, covenants, restrictions, easements and charges dated the _____ day of _____, executed by _____ Company as Declarant, and recorded in the office of the County Recorder of the County of _____, State of _____, on the _____ day of _____ _____, in Volume _____ of Official Records at page _____ thereof, the terms of office of all members of the Board of Directors of this corporation shall cease and terminate at the date of the first annual meeting of the members thereafter, and thereupon a new board of directors shall be elected by the members of this corporation at a special meeting of the members called for that purpose.

ARTICLE VII.

Vacancies

Section 1—Vacancies in the Board of Directors shall be filled by a majority of the remaining directors though less than a quorum, and each director so elected shall hold office until his successor is elected at an annual meeting or at a special meeting called for that purpose. If any director at any time tenders his resignation to the Board of Directors, the Board of Directors shall have power to elect his successor to take effect at such time as the resignation becomes effective.

ARTICLE VIII.

Powers of Directors

Section 1—The Board of Directors shall have power:

(a) To call special meetings of the members whenever it deems it necessary, and it shall call a meeting at any time upon written request of the members who have the right to vote at least one-third of all of the votes of the entire membership.

(b) To appoint and remove at pleasure all officers, agents and employees of the corporation, prescribe their duties, fix their compensation, and require from them security or a fidelity bond for faithful performance of the duties to be prescribed for them.

(c) To conduct, manage and control the affairs and business of this corporation, and to make rules and regulations not inconsistent with the laws of the State of _____ or the By-Laws of this corporation for the guidance of the officers and management of the affairs of the corporation.

(d) To establish, levy and assess, and collect the charges or assessments referred to in Article II hereof, and to fix the rate per square foot for such charges or assessments within any proper limitation.

(e) To exercise for the corporation all powers, duties and authorities vested in or delegated to this corporation or which it may lawfully exercise.

ARTICLE IX.

Duties of Directors

Section 1—It shall be the duty of the Board of Directors:

(a) To cause to be kept a complete record of all of their minutes and acts, and of the proceedings of the members, and present a full statement at the regular annual meeting of the members, showing in detail the assets and liabilities of this corporation, and generally the condition of its affairs. A similar statement shall be presented at any other meeting of the members when required by members who have the right to vote at least one-third of all the votes of the entire membership.

(b) To supervise all officers, agents and employees of this corporation, and to see that their duties are properly performed.

ARTICLE X.

Directors' Meetings

Section 1—The annual meeting of the Board of Directors shall be held on the second Monday in February of each year at the hour of 9:00 o'clock P. M.

Section 2—A regular meeting of the Board of Directors shall be held on the second Monday of each month at 2:30 o'clock P. M., provided that the Board of Directors may, by resolution, change the day and hour of holding such regular meetings.

Section 3—Notice of such annual meeting and such regular meeting is hereby dispensed with. If the day for the annual or regular meeting shall fall upon a holiday, the meeting shall be held at the same hour on the first day following which is not a holiday, and no notice thereof need be given.

Section 4—Special meetings of the Board of Directors shall be held when called by the President, the Vice-President, or Secretary or Treasurer, or upon the written request of any two directors. Written notice of each special meeting of the Board of Directors shall be delivered personally to the directors, or given or sent to each director, at least three days before the time for holding said meeting, by letter, postage thereon fully prepaid addressed to the director. Each director shall register his address with the Secretary, and notices of meetings shall be mailed to him at such address.

Section 5—The transactions of any meetings of the Board of Directors, however called and noticed, or wherever held, shall be as valid as though had at a meeting duly held after regular call and notice if a quorum be present, and if either before or after the meeting each of the directors not present sign a written waiver of notice, or a consent to holding such meeting, or an approval of the minutes thereof. All such waivers, consents or approvals shall be filed with the corporate records and made a part of the minutes of the meeting.

Section 6—Every act, or decision, done or made by a majority of the directors present at a meeting duly held at which a quorum is present shall be regarded as the act of the Board of Directors. In the absence of a quorum, the majority of the directors present may adjourn from time to time until the time fixed for the next regular meeting of the Board.

ARTICLE XI.

Meetings of Members

Section 1—The regular annual meeting of the members shall be held on the second Monday of the month of February in each year, at the hour of 8:00 o'clock P. M. If the day for the annual meeting of the members shall fall upon a holiday, the meeting shall be held at the same hour on the first day following which is not a holiday.

Section 2—Special meetings of the members for any purpose may be called at any time by the President, the Vice-President, the Secretary, the Treasurer, or by the Board of Directors, or by any two or more members thereof, or upon written request of the members who

184

have the right to vote at least one-third of all of the votes of the entire membership.

Section 3—Notices of annual and special meetings shall be given in writing to the members by the Secretary. Notice may be given to the members either personally, or by sending a copy of the notice through the mail, postage thereon fully prepaid to his address appearing on the books of the corporation. Each member shall register his address with the Secretary and notices of meetings shall be mailed to him at such address. Written notice of each meeting shall, at least three days before the time for holding said meeting, be given or sent to each member by letter, postage thereon fully prepaid addressed to the member. Notice of each annual or special meeting of the members shall specify the place, the date, and the hour of the meeting, and the general nature of the business to be transacted.

Section 4—The transactions at any meeting of the members however called or noticed shall be as valid as though had at a meeting duly held after regular call and notice if a quorum be present, in person or by proxy, if either before or after the meeting each member entitled to vote not present signs a written waiver of notice, or a consent to the holding of such meeting, or approval of the minutes thereof. All such waivers, consents or approvals shall be filed with the corporate records and made a part of the minutes of the meeting. The presence in person or by proxy of a majority of the members of this corporation shall constitute a quorum for the transaction of business. In the absence of a quorum any meeting of the members may be adjourned from time to time by a vote of a majority of the members present, but no other business may be transacted. Members present at any duly called or held meeting at which a quorum is present in person or by proxy may continue to do business notwithstanding the withdrawal of enough members to leave less than a quorum.

ARTICLE XII.
Officers

Section 1—The officers of this corporation shall be a President, a Vice-President, who shall at all times be members of the Board of Directors, and a Secretary, and a Treasurer, and such other officers as the Board of Directors may, from time to time, by resolution, create.

Section 2—The officers of this corporation, except such officers as may be appointed in accordance with Sections 3 or 5 of this Article, shall be chosen annually by the Board of Directors, and each shall hold his office for one year unless he shall sooner resign or shall be removed, or otherwise disqualified to serve.

Section 3—The Board of Directors may appoint such other officers as the business of the corporation may require, each of whom shall hold office for such period, have such authority, and perform such duties as the Board of Directors may, from time to time, determine.

Section 4—Any officer may be removed from office either with or without cause by a majority of the Directors at time in office at any annual, regular or special meeting of the Board. Any officer may resign at any time by giving a written notice to the Board of Directors, or to the President, or the Secretary of the corporation. Any such resignation shall take effect at the date of receipt of such notice, or at any later time specified therein, and unless otherwise specified therein the acceptance of such resignation shall not be necessary to make it effective.

Section 5—A vacancy in any office because of death, resignation, removal, disqualification, or other cause shall be filled in the manner prescribed in the By-Laws for regular appointment to such office.

Section 6—The offices of Secretary or Assistant-Secretary, and Treasurer may be held by the same person.

ARTICLE XIII.
President

Section 1—The Board of Directors shall at their first regular meeting elect one of their number to act as President, and shall also at said meeting elect a Vice-President.

Section 2—If at any time the President shall be unable to act, the Vice-President shall take his place and perform his duties. If the Vice-President, for any cause, shall be unable to act the Board of Directors shall appoint some member of the Board to act, in whom shall be vested for the time being all the duties and functions of the President.

Section 3—The President, or the Vice-President, or in the absence or inability to act of both the President and the Vice-President, the Director appointed as above provided

(a) Shall preside over all meetings of the members and of the Board of Directors.

(b) Shall sign as President all deeds, contracts and other instruments in writing which have been first approved by the Board of Directors.

(c) Shall call the Directors together whenever he deems it necessary and shall have, subject to the advice of the Board of Directors, general supervision, direction and control of the business affairs of the corporation, and generally shall discharge such other duties as may be required of him by the Board of Directors.

ARTICLE XIV.
Vice-President

Section 1—All duties and powers required by law, or by these By-Laws of, and all powers conferred by law or by these By-Laws upon, the President shall, in his absence, inability or refusal to act be performed by the Vice-President.

ARTICLE XV.
Secretary and Assistant-Secretary

Section 1—The Board of Directors shall elect a Secretary, and it shall be the duty of the Secretary

(a) To keep a record of all meetings and proceedings of the Board of Directors, and of the members.

(b) To keep the corporate seal of the corporation, and to affix it on all papers requiring the seal of the corporation.

(c) To keep proper books.

(d) To serve notices of meetings of the Board of Directors and the members required either by law or by the By-Laws of this corporation.

(e) To keep appropriate records showing the members of this corporation together with their addresses as furnished him by such members.

Section 2—The Board of Directors may appoint an Assistant Secretary who, in case of the absence, inability or refusal to act of the Secretary shall perform the duties of the Secretary.

Section 3—The Assistant-Secretary shall also perform such other duties as may be required of him by the Board of Directors.

ARTICLE XVI.

Treasurer

Section 1—The Treasurer shall receive and deposit in such bank or banks as the Board of Directors may, from time to time, direct, all of the funds of the corporation, which funds shall be withdrawn by such officer or officers as the Board of Directors shall, from time to time, designate.

ARTICLE XVII.

Books and Papers

Section 1—The books, records and such papers as may be placed on file by the vote of the members or the Board of Dirctors shall at all times, during reasonable business hours, be subject to the inspection of any member.

ARTICLE XVIII.

Proxies

Section 1—At all corporate meetings of members, each member may vote in person or by proxy.

Section 2—All proxies shall be in writing, and filed with the Secretary.

ARTICLE XIX.

Corporate Seal

Section 1—This corporation shall have a seal in circular form having within its circumference the words

"_____" HOMES ASSOCIATION

Incorporated _____

_____

(State)

ARTICLE XX.

Amendments

Section 1—By-Laws may be adopted, amended, or repealed

(a) By the Board of Directors, subject always to the power of the members to change or repeal such By-Laws; or

(b) By the vote or written assent of a majority of the members entitled to vote, or the vote of a majority of a quorum at a meeting duly called for such purpose.

Above By-Laws prepared by Mason-McDuffie Company, Inc., Berkeley, California.

Appendix E [1]
TABLE I
AVERAGE EXPENDITURES PER U. S. FAMILY BY PERCENTAGE

Income Level	Food	Shelter	Clothing	Transportation	Other
Under $ 500	43.6	33.5	7.5	3.9	11.5
$ 500—$ 750	43.8	32.0	7.9	4.7	11.6
$ 750—$ 1,000	41.5	32.2	8.5	5.8	12.0
$ 1,000—$ 1,250	38.4	32.9	8.9	7.2	12.6
$ 1,250—$ 1,500	36.9	32.4	9.3	8.2	13.2
$ 1,500—$ 1,750	34.9	32.3	9.7	9.2	13.9
$ 1,750—$ 2,000	33.1	32.9	9.7	10.3	14.0
$ 2,000—$ 2,500	31.4	32.4	10.5	11.3	14.4
$ 2,500—$ 3,000	30.0	32.5	11.1	11.5	14.9
$ 3,000—$ 4,000	28.2	33.2	11.6	11.7	15.3
$ 4,000—$ 5,000	26.0	33.0	12.5	12.8	15.7
$ 5,000—$10,000	23.3	34.2	12.5	12.8	17.2
$10,000—$15,000	19.9	35.9	13.6	13.1	17.5
$15,000—$20,000	19.6	32.2	13.8	14.5	19.9
$20,000 and over	15.3	36.2	14.7	14.7	19.1
All Levels	33.6	33.0	10.1	9.4	13.9

National Resources Planning Board, 1935-36.

TABLE II
AVERAGE EXPENDITURES PER U. S. FAMILY IN DOLLARS

Income Level	Food	Shelter	Clothing	Transportation	Other
$1000—$1250	$433	$371	$100	$ 81	$142
1250— 1500	487	427	123	107	172
1500— 1750	527	489	147	139	210
1750— 2000	558	556	164	172	234
2000— 2500	617	638	207	222	284
2500— 3000	690	748	255	266	343
3000— 4000	770	906	316	320	417
4000— 5000	852	1081	408	417	518
5000—10000	1038	1526	557	570	763

AMOUNT SPENT PER AVERAGE FAMILY PER YEAR FOR SPECIAL ITEMS

Beauty Parlor	$ 50.00
Clothes	150.00
Laundry	40.00
Medical	100.00
Movies	40.00
Telephone	18.00
Rugs & Curtains	10.00
Shoe Repair	6.00

National Resources Planning Board, 1935-36.

[1] Statistics appearing in Appendices E to H are reproduced here for the reader's general information, and should not be followed too closely as conditions existing in his locality at any given time may vary widely from those shown.

Appendix F

TABLE I

PERCENTAGE OF TOTAL U. S. RETAIL SALES MADE BY SELECTED KINDS OF BUSINESS

Food store _____ 25.2%
Country general stores _____ 3.4%
General merchandising _____ 13.9%
Automotive sales _____ 13.9%
Apparel stores _____ 8.0%
Furniture & household
    furnishings _____ 3.9%
Other _____ 31.7%

                                100%

TYPES OF RETAIL VOLUME DISTRIBUTED BY VARIOUS OPERATIONS

Independents _____ 73.1%
Chain groups _____ 22.8%
Others _____ 4.1%

U. S. Census Bureau, 1935.

TABLE II

TABLE OF FAMILY EXPENDITURES OF LOW INCOME GROUPS

Rent _____ 20% of income
Savings, insurance, dependents, etc. ____ 10% of income
All living expenses _____ 70% of income

DISTRIBUTION OF LIVING EXPENSES

Feeding _____	45%
Merchandise _____	14%
Clothes _____	14%
Car _____	7%
Filling Stations _____	2%
Furniture _____	1%
Hardware _____	2%
Drugs and Cosmetics _____	7%
Restaurant and Bar _____	7%
Others _____	1%
	100%

THE 45% FEEDING ITEM ABOVE IS THEN BROKEN DOWN AS FOLLOWS:

Candy _____	4.0%
Dairy products _____	6.2%
Delicatessen _____	1.7%
Fruit and vegetables _____	3.2%
Dry groceries _____	14.3%
Canned groceries _____	6.1%
Meat _____	8.3%
Bakery _____	1.0%
Others _____	.2%
	45.0%

Compiled by the Public Buildings Administration for Defense Housing Projects, 1941.

TABLE III

PERCENTAGE DISTRIBUTION OF ESTIMATED CONSUMPTION EXPENDITURES, 1950 AND 1960, WITH EXPENDITURES FOR 1940

	1940	1950	1960
Total Consumption Expenditures	100.00%	100.00%	100.00%
A. Food, Liquor, and Tobacco	30.98	31.16	_30.62
Food and Beverages	28.26	28.52	28.03
Tobacco and Smoking Supplies	2.72	2.64	2.59
B. Clothing, Accessories, and Personal Care	13.89	14.02	13.93
Clothing and Related	12.32	12.41	12.30
Personal Care	1.57	1.61	1.63
C. Housing	17.81	16.59	15.92
Rent and Imputed Rent	12.94	12.05	11.51
Fuel and Lighting Supplies	2.34	2.16	2.06
Household Utilities	2.53	2.38	2.35
D. Household Equipment and Operation	12.38	12.96	13.02
Furniture, etc.	5.23	5.56	5.64
Mechanical Appliances	1.36	1.59	1.73
Domestic Service	1.53	1.64	1.64
Communication	1.25	1.24	1.23
Cleaning, Repair, and Maintenance	1.14	1.19	1.19
Financial and Legal Expenses	1.87	1.73	1.59
E. Consumer Transportation	10.40	10.88	12.20
Private	8.07	8.25	9.42
Public Carrier	2.33	2.63	2.79
F. Medical, Insurance, and Death Expenses	6.69	6.59	6.50
Medical	4.05	4.05	4.03
Insurance	1.94	1.90	1.85
Death Expenses	.70	.64	.61
G. Recreation	4.63	4.90	5.10
Theaters, Amusements, etc.	1.23	1.27	1.35
Spectator Sports	.13	.15	.15
Reading, Hobbies, Pets	.95	.99	1.00
Organizations and Clubs	.33	.26	.22
Participant Recreation	.45	.51	.57
Radio, Television, and Music	.84	.94	1.02
Sports Equipment	.70	.77	.79
H. Private Education	1.60	1.53	1.47
Organized Education	.86	.83	.80
Unorganized Education	.74	.70	.67
I. Religion and Private Social Welfare	1.62	1.37	1.23
Religious Bodies	1.01	.87	.79
Social Welfare	.61	.50	.45

From "America's Needs and Resources", Twentieth Century Fund Survey, 1947.

Appendix G

POPULATION REQUIREMENTS OF RETAIL STORES

An idea of the number of people required to support different types of retail stores may be gathered from the data gathered by the *U. S. Census Bureau*, showing the population per store in eleven typical cities: Atlanta, Baltimore, Denver, Fargo, Kansas City, Providence, San Francisco, Seattle, Springfield (Ill.), Syracuse and Chicago.

Kind of Business	Inhabitants per Store
Art and Antique	13,371 persons
Automobile	6,673
Automobile Accessory	3,270
Bakery	2,548
Boot and Shoe	3,346
Building Material	6,960
Cigar and Tobacco	2,071
Clothing and Furnishing, Men's Ready-to-wear	2,397
Clothing, Women's	4,063
Confectionery, Ice Cream, Soft Drink	1,017
Custom Tailor	4,245
Dairy and Poultry Products	11,772
Department	53,486
Drug	1,545
Dry Goods and Notions	2,065
Electrical Appliance and Supply	9,057
Florist	2,510
Fur and Fur Clothing	19,118
Furniture and House Furnishing	2,388
Gasoline and Oil	1,643
General	90,569
Grocery, Delicatessen	325
Hardware	2,748
Hat and Cap—Men's and Boy's	26,638
Jewelry	4,958
Junk	36,131
Meat—Poultry and Fish	1,189
Millinery and Artificial Flowers	6,136
Motorcycle and Bicycle	57,565
Musical Instrument and Sheet Music	12,239
Office Equipment	15,473
Optical Goods	26,995
Paint, Oil, Varnish and Glass	11,772
Photographic Supply and Camera	63,483
Plumbing and Heating Fixture and Supply	9,447
Radio	18,306
Restaurants	813
Sporting Goods	44,985
Stationery, Books, Magazines, etc.	6,402
Toy and Games	83,860
Trunks and Leather Goods	21,227
Typewriting and Calculating Machines	40,193
Variety	18,610

U. S. Census, 1928. (Latest available Census Figures.)

Appendix H

TABLE I

VARIOUS METHODS USED IN DETERMINING SIZE OF SHOPPING CENTER

1. No. of Linear Feet of Business Frontage for Each 100 Persons
(or each 30 families)

The following figures have been given by various authorities, as the result of individual surveys and findings:

	Per 100 Persons
SOUTHERN CALIFORNIA	40′ to 60′
39 ST. LOUIS SUBURBAN AREAS (average)	61.54′
West Coast WAR HOUSING PROJECTS	25′
MEASURED PLANS	6.5′ to 27′
RECENT PUBLISHED STATEMENTS	2′ to 5′

Obviously there is no established standard of frontage measure; however, it would appear that a figure varying from *twenty to thirty* feet of business frontage per *100 persons,* depending on the size of the project, might be used as a very general guide in planning for average outlying centers.

2. AREA OF STORES PER EACH ONE THOUSAND PERSONS (300 Families)

Figures used in this method of calculation, for floor areas of stores, vary as follows:

SOUTHERN CALIFORNIA

Minor Business Centers 1.19 acres per 1000 Persons.

Secondary Business Centers 2.11 acres per 1000 Persons.

Complete Business Centers 2.75 acres per 1000 Persons.

A WAR HOUSING STANDARD

A Community of 1000 Persons, 0.16 acres.

A Community of 3000 Persons, 0.14 acres per 1000.

A Community of 5000 Persons, 0.12 acres per 1000.

Measurements of a selected number of representative shopping centers averaged 0.81 acres per 1000 Persons.

For a rough estimate, a liberal figure of *one acre of stores for each 1000 persons* may be used if checked by other methods.

3. PERCENT OF TOTAL AREA OF COMMUNITY FOR BUSINESS USE.

Examination of a number of outlying neighborhood developments and self-contained communities has shown a range from 1.5% to 2.38% and 2.5% of total gross area used for business.

This method might be applied in a broad sense to certain small towns and cities, but is not useable in measuring the requirements for setting up a shopping center.

4. POTENTIAL PURCHASING POWER.

Potential purchasing power is based on the percentage of family incomes spent for household and personal commodities and services. It is estimated that individual families expend approximately 70% of their incomes for living expenses. This figure by reference to statistical tables may be broken down into specific amounts spent locally for ordinary items. Given these figures it is possible to determine the number and kinds of businesses which may reasonably be expected to operate successfully in a given neighborhood.

193

5. ADDITIONAL DATA.

Reference tables and data are available which give approximately the number of consumers in a neighborhood necessary for the support of all types of stores. Similar figures are also given for the number of stores which different size communities will require.

No single method as stated above is sufficient in itself to scientifically plan a shopping center. Only through a collective application of various methods may a satisfactory program be derived.

The successful shopping center is one which works, and the one which works is one which in the end supplies the particular needs of its own individual community.

TABLE II
AVERAGE USEABLE DIMENSIONS AND AREAS FOR TYPES OF RETAIL STORES IN LARGE SUBURBAN CENTERS

	Dimensions	Area
1. Super Market	120' x 200'	24,000 sq. ft.
2. Food Market (Chain)	100' x 125'	12,500 sq. ft.
3. Theater	60' x 150'	10,000 sq. ft.
4. Food Market (Independent)	50' x 100'	5,000 sq. ft.
5. Department Store	50' x 100'	5,000 sq. ft.
6. Five and Ten (Chain)	50' x 100'	5,000 sq. ft.
7. Drug Store (Chain)	40' x 100'	4,000 sq. ft.
8. Variety—Junior Department	35' x 90'	3,150 sq. ft.
9. Ladies Wear	30' x 100'	3,000 sq. ft.
10. Drug Store (Independent)	30' x 90'	2,700 sq. ft.
11. Restaurant and Bar	25' x 100'	2,500 sq. ft.
12. Shoes	25' x 100'	2,500 sq. ft.
13. Bank	30' x 75'	2,250 sq. ft.
14. Hardware	30' x 70'	2,100 sq. ft.
15. Furniture	30' x 70'	2,100 sq. ft.
16. Meat Market	35' x 50'	1,750 sq. ft.
17. Men's Wear	25' x 70'	1,750 sq. ft.
18. Ladies' Hat Shop	25' x 70'	1,750 sq. ft.
19. Tea Room, etc.	25' x 50'	1,250 sq. ft.
20. Liquor Store	15' x 75'	1,125 sq. ft.
21. Post Office	25' x 50'	1,250 sq. ft.
22. Jewelry (Watch Repair)	15' x 75'	1,125 sq. ft.
23. Bakery	15' x 70'	1,050 sq. ft.
24. Dry Cleaning and Dyeing	15' x 70'	1,050 sq. ft.
25. Laundry (Pick-up)	15' x 70'	1,050 sq. ft.
26. Delicatessen	15' x 70'	1,050 sq. ft.
27. Radios and Repair and Electric	15' x 70'	1,050 sq. ft.
28. Candy and Ice Cream	20' x 50'	1,000 sq. ft.
29. Florist	15' x 50'	750 sq. ft.
30. Barber	15' x 50'	750 sq. ft.
31. Beauty Parlor	15' x 50'	750 sq. ft.
32. Cigar and Tobacco	15' x 50'	750 sq. ft.
33. Book and Stationery Store	12' x 50'	600 sq. ft.
34. Shoe Repair	15' x 34'	510 sq. ft.
35. Gift Shop	15' x 30'	450 sq. ft.

These figures have been taken from existing stores and store plans of recent construction. Obviously under special conditions any of these businesses may operate in considerably less space. The even widths and depths shown are not recommended by the Community Builders' Council. See discussion of store sizes on page 152.

No builder should be guided blindly by the above areas and dimensions, but rather, should study his own situation carefully. For instance, Items 1, 12, 18, 24, 25, and 32 are considered too large by some Council members, while Items 5, 15, 17, and 27 are considered too small.

Appendix I

TYPES OF SHOPS BY SIZE OF SHOPPING CENTER [1]

"I have endeavored below to make a suggested grouping of logical shops, first for a small suburban business center, second for a medium sized business center, and third for a large suburban business center.

"In making the following grouping, I wish to emphasize that it is not possible to lay down any hard and fast rules. In various cities and even in various centers in the same city, careful consideration must be given to the very great difference in buying power and habits in the community; distance from the downtown business area; topography; size of possible contributing trade area; automobile or bus and street car transportation; merchandising ability of particular merchants; the possible grouping of shops that can be created in a particular center thereby favorably affecting the volume of shops that otherwise could not succeed; the success of stores that are branches of well known downtown stores as compared with new independent stores of the same type; distance from competing centers; amount of nearby walk-in trade; parking facilities available; amount of nearby office population, and many other factors must be considered.

"I want to point out that the grouping of shops in the center by type is of very great importance in bringing about related buying."

J. C. NICHOLS.

NUMBER ONE

10 OR 15 TYPES THAT ARE RECOMMENDED FOR A SMALL CENTER

Drugstore	Barber shop
Service grocery store	Shoe repair shop
Cash and carry grocery	Cleaner & Dyer & Laundry
Bakery	Beauty shop
Small notion or variety store	Filling station

NUMBER TWO

15 TO 50 SHOPS—IN ADDITION TO ABOVE FOR A MEDIUM SIZED CENTER

An additional drugstore (one chain and one personally owned)	Stationery and book store with rental library
	Photographer
Cash and carry grocery (large)	Restaurant or cafe
Service grocery	Frozen food rental lockers, perhaps including sale of frozen food
Liquor Store	
Popular priced dress shop	
Haberdasher	Fixit shop
Millinery shop	Ice cream, candy and nut shop
Another beauty shop	Dentists
Small five and ten cent store	Physicians

---

[1] Prepared for the Community Builders' Council, February 4, 1946.

15 TO 50 SHOPS—IN ADDITION TO ABOVE FOR A MEDIUM SIZED CENTER (Continued)

Electrical supply and repair shop with radio
Shoe store
Gift shop
Florist

Another filling station
Motion picture theater
Garage
Baby shop
Athletic goods

NUMBER THREE

LARGER CENTERS—50 TO 100 OR MORE TENANTS—IN ADDITION TO ABOVE

Several ladies apparel shops
Fur shop and fur storage
Corset shop
Girls' clothing shop
Lingerie and hosiery shops
Hemstitching and button making shop
Needle work and knit shop
Maternity apparel shop
More dressmakers
Jewelry store and watch repair
Dry goods store
Tailors, both men's and women's
Specialized shoe stores
Fruit and vegetable shop
Large food markets
Two service groceries
Delicatessen
Meat market
More beauty parlors
Cosmetic shop
Large restaurant
Cafeteria
Tea Room
Stationery and greeting card shop
Rug and drapery shop
Furniture and carpet store
Linen Shop
Importer's shop such as Chinese, Mexican, or Indian merchandise
Upholsterer
Antique shop
China and glassware
Interior decorating shops
Second hand furniture shop (In some areas)
Plumbing supplies and display room

Dental laboratory
Osteopath and chiropractor
Nurses' registry
Christian Science practitioners and reading room
Men's clothing store
Boys' clothing shop
Woolworth, Kresge, or other types of 10c store
Department store, and such stores as Sears Roebuck or Montgomery Ward
Firestone type of store
Candy shops
Popcorn and nut shop
Restaurant and Bar
Bottled liquor stores
Hardware and key shop
House appliance store (possibly combine with hardware store)
Play equipment and hobby shop
Toy shop
Lighting fixtures (doubtful)
Sheet music and musical instruments (doubtful)
Music studios
Dancing schools
Business schools
Public accountant
Public stenographer
Advertising agency
Attorney
Travel bureau, l u g g a g e and leather goods
Western Auto store
Sewing machine agencies
Print shop
Letter shop
Bowling alleys and billiard parlor

197

Bird and pet shop and supplies

Camera shop, photographic and moving picture equipment

Phonograph and record shop

Sporting goods shop

Picture framing shop

Paint and wall paper shop

Photograph galleries

Physicians and dentists of all types

Optometrists

Optical shop

More filling stations

Another garage

Automobile agencies

Bank and safety deposit vault

Post office

Express office

Telegraph office

Service companies, such as telephone, gas and electric companies

Pharmacy and prescription shop

Art studio

As a center grows in size, you should constantly shift the locations of various types of businesses in order to improve the grouping of related shops and free the "hot spot" locations for higher rental shops and more intensive uses.

Index

199

Utility companies, private, 17
  construction, 76-81
  services in site selection, 15

V

Valuation of improved land, Table 3,
  p. 14
Views, value of, 19

W

Walking distance to employment, 5
Walstrom, C. R., 75
Washington, D. C., Naylor Road Shopping Center, Plate XII, 112, 113
Waste disposal, 26
Water, companies, community, 16; co-
  operatives, 16
  distributing system, central supply,
  fire protection, location of mains,
  private supply, 81
  mains, availability of, 15; quantity
  and pressure, 16
  public supply, 16
  service, revenue from, 17
  storm, 16
Wells, individual, 16

Wenzlick, Roy, & Co., 21
Westchester, Business Center, Los
  Angeles, Cal., 118-122
Westwood Village, Los Angeles, Cali-
  fornia, 155
Whitten and Adams, 14
Willmore, Cyrus Crane, 13, 19
Winter, Foster, 117
Woodside Hills, plat of survey, San
  Mateo County, California, 6
Worthington, Hayden, 121

Z

Zoning boards, 1, 4
  Boards of Appeal, 104
  business, 103
  county, 27
  economic factors, 27
  nature and status of, 26
  applied to parking, 103
  relation to protective covenants,
  27, 85
  revisions in, 27
  adjacent to site, 17
  weaknesses of, 27

PRESS OF BYRON S. ADAMS
WASHINGTON, D. C.

ISBN 0-87420-844-0